Multimedia Information Retrieval

Multimedia Information Retrieval

Stefan Rüger

ISBN: 978-3-031-01141-2   paperback
ISBN: 978-3-031-02269-2   ebook

DOI 10.1007/978-3-031-02269-2

A Publication in the Springer series
SYNTHESIS LECTURES ON INFORMATION CONCEPTS, RETRIEVAL, AND SERVICES

Lecture #10
Series Editor: Gary Marchionini, *University North Carolina, Chapel Hill*
Series ISSN
Synthesis Lectures on Information Concepts, Retrieval, and Services
Print 1947-945X   Electronic 1947-9468

Synthesis Lectures on Information Concepts, Retrieval, and Services

Editor
Gary Marchionini, *University North Carolina, Chapel Hill*

Multimedia Information Retrieval
Stefan Rüger
2009

Information Architecture: The Design and Integration of Information Spaces
Wei Ding, Xia Lin
2009

Reading and Writing the Electronic Book
Catherine C. Marshall
2009

Hypermedia Genes: An Evolutionary Perspective on Concepts, Models, and Architectures
Nuno M. Guimarães, Luís M. Carriço
2009

Understanding User-Web Interactions via Web Analytics
Bernard J. (Jim) Jansen
2009

XML Retrieval
Mounia Lalmas
2009

Faceted Search
Daniel Tunkelang
2009

Introduction to Webometrics: Quantitative Web Research for the Social Sciences
Michael Thelwall
2009

Exploratory Search: Beyond the Query-Response Paradigm
Ryen W. White, Resa A. Roth
2009

New Concepts in Digital Reference
R. David Lankes
2009

Automated Metadata in Multimedia Information Systems: Creation, Refinement, Use in Surrogates, and Evaluation
Michael G. Christel
2009

Multimedia Information Retrieval

Stefan Rüger
The Open University

SYNTHESIS LECTURES ON INFORMATION CONCEPTS, RETRIEVAL, AND SERVICES #10

ABSTRACT

At its very core multimedia information retrieval means the process of searching for and finding multimedia documents; the corresponding research field is concerned with building the best possible multimedia search engines. The intriguing bit here is that the query itself can be a multimedia excerpt: For example, when you walk around in an unknown place and stumble across an interesting landmark, would it not be great if you could just take a picture with your mobile phone and send it to a service that finds a similar picture in a database and tells you more about the building — and about its significance for that matter?

This book goes further by examining the full matrix of a variety of query modes versus document types. How do you retrieve a music piece by humming? What if you want to find news video clips on forest fires using a still image? The text discusses underlying techniques and common approaches to facilitate multimedia search engines from metadata driven retrieval, via piggy-back text retrieval where automated processes create text surrogates for multimedia, automated image annotation and content-based retrieval. The latter is studied in great depth looking at features and distances, and how to effectively combine them for efficient retrieval, to a point where the readers have the ingredients and recipe in their hands for building their own multimedia search engines.

Supporting users in their resource discovery mission when hunting for multimedia material is not a technological indexing problem alone. We look at interactive ways of engaging with repositories through browsing and relevance feedback, roping in geographical context, and providing visual summaries for videos. The book concludes with an overview of state-of-the-art research projects in the area of multimedia information retrieval, which gives an indication of the research and development trends and, thereby, a glimpse of the future world.

KEYWORDS

multimedia information retrieval, multimedia digital libraries, visual search, content-based retrieval, piggy-back text retrieval, automated image annotation, audiovisual fingerprinting, semantic gap, polysemy, multimedia features and distances, fusion of features and distances, high-dimensional indexing, video summaries, information visualisation, relevance feedback, geo-temporal browsing

Contents

Preface

I am not easily convinced to write a book. The main reason why I got fascinated by this assignment is that it gave me a unique opportunity to write up tricks of the trade that are relevant for a number of multimedia search projects (and that I have had to endlessly repeat, again and again, during the supervision of around 65 undergraduate, master and PhD projects over the last decade). The Morgan & Claypool format of this lecture series is great too, as I can go to considerably more detail than in a book chapter without having to deliver a 700 page opus.

This book targets undergraduate classes on multimedia information retrieval, and everyone who carries out projects that build components of multimedia search for work or studies, in particular for individual final projects — be it at undergraduate or graduate level. I have put an emphasis on illustrating the material with figures, photographs and videos, but also gone to the technical depth of explicit mathematical relations that form the core of the technologies. Each theme is cross-referenced to a set of relevant and significant primary literature, which will help readers along who wish to delve into even more detail. Each chapter concludes with a set of reflective exercises, which can be used as supplemental assignments for university courses or as suggestions for further independent exploration by interested readers.

I know that this book will save me and my students much time and effort in the future, and I hope that others can benefit from it, too.

Stefan Rüger
November 2009

CHAPTER 1

What is Multimedia Information Retrieval?

1.1 INFORMATION RETRIEVAL

We all have come to experience information retrieval as a process that involves search engines, for example, Google, Yahoo, Microsoft's Bing and many more. Giving users access to documents is one of the defining tasks of information retrieval. For thousands of years, the traditional methods of information retrieval have been facilitated by librarians: they create reference cards with metadata that are put into catalogues (nowadays databases); they also place the objects in physical locations that follow certain classification schemes, and they answer questions at the reference desk.

One of the oldest documented instances of "information retrieval" arose for cuneiform clay tablets from the cradle of civilisation in Mesopotamia. These tablets recorded business accounts and religious texts, and they were kept at the time for later reference. Figure 1.1 is a wonderful example of such a clay tablet from the 24th century BCE, now in the Kirkor Minassian collection in the Library of Congress.

Figure 1.1: Clay tablet

Hundreds of thousands of these tablets survived war, conflict and burning down of libraries and temples. Actually, the fire may have preserved more of the tablets than was intended at the time! They were usually kept in storerooms full of boxes. Apart from the fact that only an elite within the population were allowed to access the tablets, the storerooms were often physically difficult to reach: located underground and sometimes only accessible by a ladder through a hole in the ceiling.

Searching for specific tablets was equally cumbersome, but at least facilitated by clay tablets that, for each of the boxes, detailed the boxes' contents. The Sumerians in ancient Iraq did not have titles on their documents: they used *incipits* instead, which are the first few words of the text. Here is an example of the incipits on one tablet (Lerner, 2001; Dalby, 1986):

1. Honored and noble warrior
2. Where are the sheep
3. Where are the wild oxen
4. And with you I did not
5. In our city
6. In former days
7. Lord of the observance of heavenly laws
8. Residence of my God
9. Gibil, Gibil [the fire god]
10. On the 30th day, the day when sleeps
11. God An [the sky god], great ruler
12. An righteous woman, who heavenly laws

Those incipit tables served as orientation for browsing and searching 5000 years ago, and still today, we use little catalogue cards with a small description of documents to facilitate finding them. In this respect, little has changed except technology. Today, rather than climbing down into storerooms and matching our information need with the incipits of the documents in boxes, we deploy computers to match our information need with the text of the documents itself.

There is no denying that the advent of digital documents has radically changed the organisation principles; now it is possible to *automatically* index and search document collections as big as the world-wide web — and browse them utilising author-inserted links. It is almost as if automated processing has turned the traditional library access paradigm upside down. Instead of searching metadata catalogues in order to retrieve the document, web search engines search the full content of documents and retrieve their metadata, eg, the location where documents can be found or the names of authors who wrote about certain themes or concepts.

How have increasing computer power and collapsing storage costs made it easy, conceptually at least, to search for text in huge collections? One simplified answer is that computers insert *every* word from the document into an index that points back to the documents. So, when we query with a single word in a web search engine, the indexing process has already created a huge list of web pages that contain this word. If we type two words into a search box, then the intersection of the two corresponding lists is returned.

The index of any web search engine looks just like the text index from the travel guide of Figure 1.2 with the differences that every word is indexed and that documents are listed instead of page numbers.

I do not want to hide the fact that there remains a large number of engineering challenges and many other research questions, too: What is the best way to rank matching documents? How to best utilise document structure? How to best express the user's information need? These research

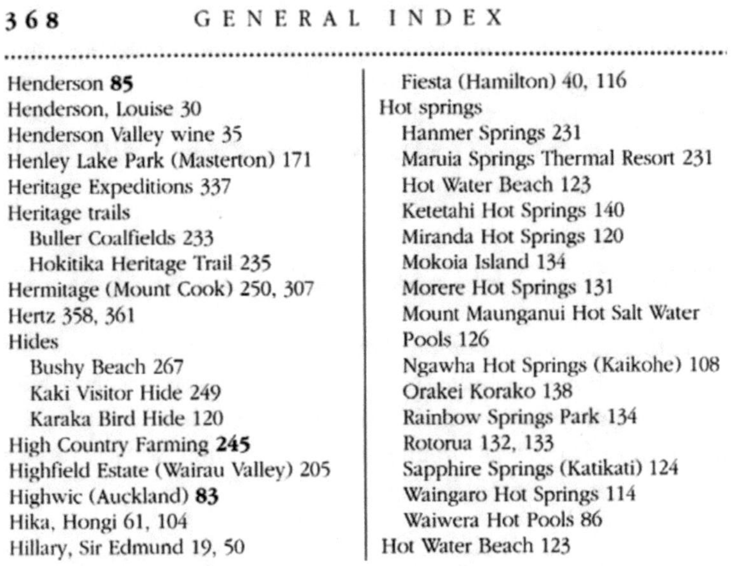
368 GENERAL INDEX

Henderson **85**
Henderson, Louise 30
Henderson Valley wine 35
Henley Lake Park (Masterton) 171
Heritage Expeditions 337
Heritage trails
  Buller Coalfields 233
  Hokitika Heritage Trail 235
Hermitage (Mount Cook) 250, 307
Hertz 358, 361
Hides
  Bushy Beach 267
  Kaki Visitor Hide 249
  Karaka Bird Hide 120
High Country Farming **245**
Highfield Estate (Wairau Valley) 205
Highwic (Auckland) **83**
Hika, Hongi 61, 104
Hillary, Sir Edmund 19, 50
  Fiesta (Hamilton) 40, 116
Hot springs
  Hanmer Springs 231
  Maruia Springs Thermal Resort 231
  Hot Water Beach 123
  Ketetahi Hot Springs 140
  Miranda Hot Springs 120
  Mokoia Island 134
  Morere Hot Springs 131
  Mount Maunganui Hot Salt Water Pools 126
  Ngawha Hot Springs (Kaikohe) 108
  Orakei Korako 138
  Rainbow Springs Park 134
  Rotorua 132, 133
  Sapphire Springs (Katikati) 124
  Waingaro Hot Springs 114
  Waiwera Hot Pools 86
Hot Water Beach 123

Figure 1.2: Index of a book

questions, and many more, are catered for by the thriving and large field of Information Retrieval, but are outside the scope of this book.

The important message here is that the combination of being digital and cheap computing power has transformed the process of information retrieval into a disruptive search technology that has given rise to a multinational multi-billion search industry.

1.2 MULTIMEDIA

Literally, the word *multimedia* means "two or more different media" and refers to different "modes" of information consumption: listening, seeing, reading, watching, smelling etc. In contrast, *monomedium* is understood to mean just one medium: a photograph, a piece of text, an audio music track, a video etc. It should be noted that videos are often subsumed under multimedia, as they have both a visual channel and an aural channel. In the same way, one might argue that newspapers constitute multimedia (as they are a mixture of text, still photographs and sketches) or, likewise, monomedia (as they *are* one object, one medium). These perspectives are further confounded by the advent of the world-wide web, which has introduced explicit and easy to follow hyperlinks between documents. The term *hypertext* refers to such interlinked text documents, while *hypermedia* refers to interlinked media. For the purpose of this book, the distinctions between these four terms (multimedia, monomedium, hypertext, hypermedia) is not relevant, and I will loosely subsume all these into multimedia.

There are two important restrictions, though, in my use of the term multimedia within this book: it needs to be *digital*, so that the processing methods detailed here can be applied, and it ought to be meant for *communication* rather than purely entertainment or art. A digitised — 3d or otherwise — scan of the cuneiform clay tablet in Figure 1.1 is considered "multimedia" in the framework of this book, the original tablet not. This book does not focus on music retrieval except in the case of symbolic score representations as these are also used for communication. Music retrieval is a large research field of its own with dedicated conferences, most notably ISMIR[1], and is, symbolic music retrieval aside, outside the scope of this book.

1.3   MULTIMEDIA INFORMATION RETRIEVAL

At its very core, multimedia information retrieval means the process of searching for and finding multimedia documents; the corresponding research field is concerned with building multimedia search engines. The intriguing bit about multimedia retrieval is that the query itself can be a multimedia excerpt: for example, if you walk around in pleasant Milton Keynes, you may stumble across the interesting building that is depicted in Figure 1.3.

Figure 1.3: Milton Keynes's Peace Pagoda

Would it not be nice if you could just take a picture with your mobile phone and send it to a service that matches your picture to their database and tells you more about the building? The service could reply with *"Built by the monks and nuns of the Nipponzan Myohoji, this was the first Peace Pagoda to be built in the western hemisphere and enshrines sacred relics of Lord Buddha. The Inauguration ceremony, on 21st September 1980, was presided over by the late most Venerable Nichidattsu Fujii, founder . . . "*[2]

---

[1] http://www.ismir.net
[2] http://www.mkweb.co.uk/places_to_visit/displayarticle.asp?id=411

Given the much wider remit of multimedia search over just text search, and assuming we could perfectly search with queries that are "multimedia" itself, what could we do with multimedia search?

The previous example is an obvious applications for tourism. There are also applications for advertising that so much seems to underpin the whole search industry: Snaptell Inc, is a startup company that specialises in mobile image search; their idea is that customers take pictures from print-media adverts, send them in and receive promotion or product information, vouchers and so on. For example, customers sending in a picture of the print poster that advertises a new movie receive an exclusive trailer, see showtimes of cinemas in the area and, in theory, could straight away phone to order tickets. One added benefit for advertisers is that they receive feedback as to where print adverts were noticed.

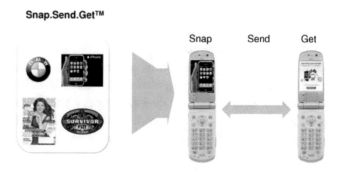

Figure 1.4: Snaptell's service

Another considerable and obvious application is for medical image databases. When someone who suffers from shortness of breath consults doctors, they might wonder where they have seen the light shadow on the x-ray before. If computers were able to match significant, medically relevant patterns with those in the database, they could return data on these diagnosed cases, so the specialists can undertake an informed differential diagnosis using medical-image retrieval (Figure 1.5).

The common factor of the previous examples was that documents and queries can consist of various different media. Figure 1.6 takes this observation radically forward by looking at the full matrix of combining different query modes (columns) with document repository types (rows). Entry A in this matrix corresponds to a traditional text search engine; this deploys a completely different technology than Entry B, a system that allows you to express musical queries by humming a tune and that then plays the corresponding song. The three C entries in Figure 1.6 correspond to a multi-modal video search engine allowing search by emotion with example images and text queries, eg, *find me video shots of "sad" scenes using an image of a dilapidated castle and the text "vampire"*. In contrast to this, Entry D could be a search engine with a query text box that returns BBC Radio 4 discussions.

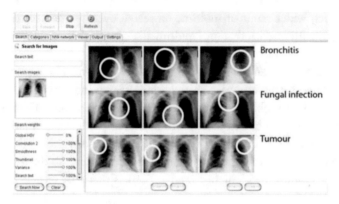

Figure 1.5: Medical-image retrieval (mock-up)

It is relatively easy to come up with a usage scenario for each of the matrix elements in Figure 1.6: for example, the image input speech output matrix element might be "given an X-ray image of a patient's chest, retrieve dictaphone documents with a relevant spoken description of a matching diagnosis". However, creating satisfying retrieval solutions is highly non-trivial and the main subject of the multimedia information retrieval discipline. Chapter 2 summarises different basic technologies involved in these multimedia search modes. Not all combinations are equally useful, desirable or well researched, though: Entry E might be a query where you roar like a lion and hope to retrieve a wildlife documentary.

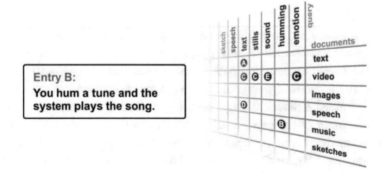

Figure 1.6: New search engine types

Undoubtedly, it is the automated approaches that have made all the difference to the way the vast collections can be used. While the automated indexing of *text* documents has been successfully applied to collections as large as the world-wide-web for nearly two decades now, multimedia indexing by content involves different, still less mature and, in some sense, less scalable technologies. One focus of this book is these automated methods known as *content-based* retrieval.

1.4 CHALLENGES OF AUTOMATED MULTIMEDIA INDEXING

Multimedia collections pose their very own challenges; for one, queries in one media mode need to be able to match potentially *other* media modes (*cross-media retrieval*). Another difficulty is that images and videos don't often come with dedicated reference cards or metadata, and when they do, as in museum collections, their creation will have been expensive and time-consuming.

There are a number of open issues with the content-based retrieval approach in multimedia. On a perceptual level, those low-level features do not necessarily correlate with any high-level meaning the images might have. This problem is known as the *semantic gap*: look at the photograph from 1966 in Figure 1.7 in which Bobby Moore, the captain of the English National Football team, receives the world cup trophy from Queen Elizabeth II. For a computer, this photograph is simply a number of pixels with a certain colour distribution. With state-of-the-art computer vision algorithms, you will detect (if not recognise) the faces, possibly even the vase-like object. But think again: this photograph depicts the captain of a national team receiving a trophy from Her Royal Highness Queen Elizabeth II for winning a world tournament in arguably the most important sport in that country! This image is really about glory, victory and triumph[3]. This discrepancy between low-level features and high-level meaning is called the semantic gap.

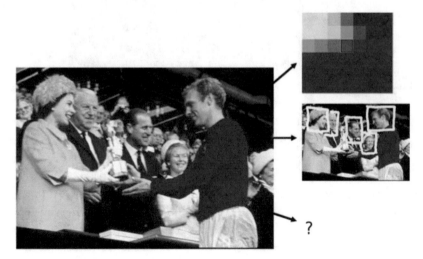

Figure 1.7: The semantic gap

---

[3]if you support the English team, that is — for supporters of the West German team, this image probably signified misery, defeat, agony and, as Reid and Zisserman (1996) proved, justified misgivings about a particular linesman decision

Some of the computer vision methods go towards the bridging of the semantic gap, for example, the ability to assign simple concrete labels to image parts such as "grass", "sky", "people", "plates". This automated annotation is the theme of Section 2.4. A consequent use of an ontology could explain the presence of higher-level concepts such as "barbecue" in terms of the simpler labels.

Even if the semantic gap could be bridged, there is still another challenge, namely *polysemy*: images usually convey a multitude of meanings so that the query-by-example approach is bound to under-specify the real information need. Users who submit an image such as the one in Figure 1.8 could have a dozen different information needs in mind: "find other images with the same person", "find images of the same art scene", "find other bright art sculptures", "find images with gradual shadow transitions", … It is these different interpretations that make further user feedback so important. Section 4.4 discusses how the explicit support of browsing processes can help leverage the intelligence of the user, specifically in the context of relevance feedback techniques that put the user in the loop and are discussed in Section 4.3.

Figure 1.8: Photographs and polysemy

On a practical level, the multitude of features assigned to images poses a *fusion problem*; how to combine possibly conflicting evidence of two images' similarity? Subsection 3.6 discusses some approaches.

There is a *responsiveness problem*, too, in that the naïve comparison of query feature vectors to the database feature vectors requires a linear scan through the database. Although the scan is eminently scalable, the practicalities of doing this operation can mean an undesirable response time in the order of 10s of seconds or worse — rather than the constant 100 milli-seconds that can be achieved by text search engines. The problem is that high-dimensional tree structures tend to be not very effective, so that compression methods or approximative nearest neighbour searches need to be deployed for efficiency. Subsection 3.5 looks into these techniques.

Even if all these challenges were solved, indexing sheer mass is no guarantee of a success-ful annotation either: while most of today's inter-library loan systems allow access to virtually any publication in the world — there are at least around 150m bibliographic entries in OCLC's Worldcat database[4], and 3m entries from Bowker's Books In Print — students and researchers alike seem to be reluctant to actually make use of this facility. On the other hand, the much smaller catalogue offered by online bookshops appears to be very popular, presumably owing to added services such as the following:

- subject categories
- fault tolerant search tools
- personalised services telling the customer what's new in a subject area
- collaborative filtering: what have others with a similar profile bought?
- pictures of book covers
- media and customer reviews
- access to the table of contents and to selections of the text
- full-text index of popular books
- the perception of fast delivery

In the same spirit, traditional search engine companies such as Google, Yahoo and Microsoft invest much of their resources into ways of keeping their market share with added functionality in almost any aspects of information management that consumers may be interested in: diaries, calendars, maps, shopping, etc.

In the multimedia context, Chapter 4 argues that automated added services such as visual queries, relevance feedback and summaries can prove useful for information retrieval in multimedia digital libraries. Section 4.1 is about summarising techniques for videos, Section 4.2 exemplifies visualisation of search results, while Section 4.3 discusses visual search modes such as query-by-example in the context of relevance feedback. Finally, Section 4.4 promotes browsing as resource discovery mode and looks at underlying techniques to automatically structure the document collection to support browsing.

The current research challenges in multimedia information retrieval are being exemplified with state-of-the-art research projects in Chapter 5.

1.5   SUMMARY

Digitisation means that we are no longer restricted to catalogue cards. We can carry out fulltext searches in books and articles with just about any keyword that we deem relevant; computers tell us who the author is, what the title is and where to find the resource. Rather than searching through catalogues to find the books, computers search through books to find their catalogue cards. Multimedia retrieval is an attempt to do the same with multimedia rather than solely text, ie, automatically index multimedia based on its contents and then use same- or cross-modal matching techniques to retrieve relevant multimedia from multimedia queries.

---

[4]http://www.oclc.org/worldcat/statistics as of Nov 2009

1.6 EXERCISES

1.6.1 MEMEX

One of the early true visionaries of digital libraries was Vannevar Bush (1890–1974): he predicted the internet and modern digital libraries long ahead of their time — and did not live to experience them! In July 1945 he published an essay "As we may think" in The Atlantic Monthly, in which he described the idea of a memory extender, short *memex*. This fictitious machine (see Figure 1.9 for its design) would be integrated into a desk that contains a glass plate with a camera to take pictures of pages, microfilm storage, projection systems for two screens, and a keyboard with levers. Its purpose was to provide scientists with the capability to exchange information and to have access to all recorded information in a private library that contained all your books, correspondence and own work. It would function as a rapid information retrieval system and extend the power of human memory.

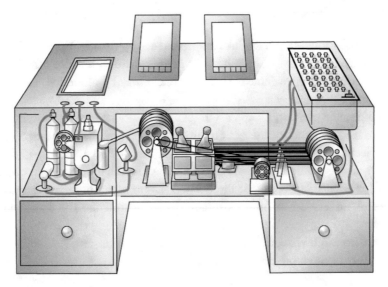

Figure 1.9: Memex design

More importantly, his design included the concept of associating resources and adding comments to them. The most remarkable fact of the memex design is that its (analogue) links are very similar to the links on web-pages. For that reason, Bush is now seen as the grandfather of the world-wide web. It took nearly two decades after the invention of the internet for the element of memex that allows adding your own work to be widely and easily used: wikipedia[5], an online encyclopedia, was born in 2001, where everyone can link to resources, add comments and corrections and write own articles.

[5] http://wikipedia.org

• Discuss whether the microfilms in the memex constitute monomedia, multimedia, hypertext or hypermedia in their strict literal sense. What about wikipedia articles? Or this book used online? What about the same as a printed book? Which of the above are multimedia as defined in Section 1.2?

1.6.2   LOOPS AND INTERACTION

Information retrieval is more than just search: it is browsing, searching, selecting, assessing and evaluating, ie, ultimately accessing information. Figure 1.10 gives a breakdown of different stages of this process from information need to information use.

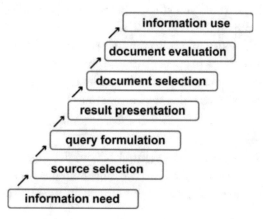

Figure 1.10: Stages of Information Retrieval

• Illustrate these steps using examples of an information retrieval quest for (a) a book, say an early "Asterix" graphic novel, in your local library; (b) for a government tax form on the web that allows you to declare the income-equivalent-benefits of your employer providing free tea; (c) for a figure in an electronic image library that demonstrates how a prism disperses light into rainbow colors.
• Identify loops in this process, for example, after document evaluation you may want to go back to the document selection step. Add all loops to Figure 1.10 that you think useful for the information retrieval process.

1.6.3   AUTOMATED VS MANUAL

Not all manual intervention has been abandoned in web search engines. For example, the Yahoo directory is an edited classification scheme of submitted web sites that are put into a browsable directory structure akin to library classification schemes.
• Find and discuss other examples of manual intervention or manually delivered services that are associated to web search engines.

1.6.4   COMPOUND TEXT QUERIES

Text search engines normally go through the following indexing steps: collect the documents to be indexed; extract a list of terms from each document by ignoring punctuation, identifying word-boundaries and normalising terms with respect to accents, diacritics spelling variants and folding to lower case; and maintain one list of documents for every term sorted by decreasing relevance. Such a list is called postings list for that particular term. The set of postings lists for the whole vocabulary is called *inverted-file index*, simply *index* or, misleadingly, *inverted index*.

• Assuming you wanted a two-term query *white house* to return all documents that contain the terms *white* and *house*, what would be a fast way of processing the intersection between the two postings lists for *white* and *house*? How would you efficiently compute the results for the query *white −house* targeting documents that contain the term *white* but not the term *house*?

• How could you change the index of a collection in order to be able to search for phrases such as *white house* requiring the two terms to appear successively in the document?

• Implement a simple text search engine that indexes e-mail folders using above ideas: relevance is defined as recency of the e-mail (the older, the less relevant).

1.6.5   SEARCH TYPES

Revisit the matrix of search engine types in Figure 1.6. Give five more search and retrieval scenarios for elements of this query-retrieval matrix. Give two more examples for search and retrieval scenarios that, like Entry C, span multiple query modes or multiple document types.

CHAPTER 2

Basic Multimedia Search Technologies

The current best practice to index multimedia collections is via the generation of a library card, ie, a dedicated database entry of metadata such as author, title, publication year and keywords. Depending on the concrete implementation, these can be found with SQL database queries, text-search engines or XML queries, but all these search modes are based on text descriptions of some form and are agnostic to the structure of the actual objects they refer to, be it books, CDs, videos, newspaper articles, paintings, sculptures, web pages, consumer products etc. The first section of this chapter is about the traditional metadata driven retrieval.

The text column of the matrix of Figure 1.6 is underpinned by text search technology and requires the textual representation of the multimedia objects, an approach that I like to call *piggy-back text retrieval*. Other approaches are based on an automatic classification of multimedia objects and on assigning words from a fixed vocabulary. This can be a certain camera motion that can be detected in a video (zoom, pan etc); a genre for music pieces such as jazz or classics; a generic scene description in images such as inside/outside, people, vegetation, landscape, grass, city-view etc or specific object detection like faces and cars etc. These approaches are known as *feature classification* or *automated annotation*.

The type of search that is most commonly associated with multimedia is *content-based*: the basic idea is that still images, music extracts, video clips themselves can be used as queries and that the retrieval system is expected to return 'similar' database entries. This technology differs most radically from the thousands-year-old library card paradigm in that there is no necessity for metadata at all. In certain searches, there is the desire to match not only the general type of scene or music that the the query represents but instead one and only one exact multimedia object. For example, you take a picture of a painting in a gallery and submit this as a query in the hope of receiving the gallery's (or otherwise) record about this particular painting. In this case, you use an image of the real world to obtain a link into the electronic world and not to see a variant or otherwise similar exhibit. The underlying technology is sometimes called *fingerprinting* or *known-item search*.

2.1   METADATA DRIVEN RETRIEVAL

Metadata are pieces of information about a multimedia object that are not strictly necessary for working with it, but that are useful to

- *describe* resources so they can be indexed, classified, located, browsed and found
- *store technical* information, such as data formats and compression schemes

- *manage* resources such as their rights or where they are currently located
- *record preservation* actions
- *create usage* trails, eg, which section of a video has been watched how many times

All of these aspects are relevant for multimedia information retrieval. Undoubtedly, the first type of so-named *descriptive metadata* has been deployed since thousands of years to keep track of documents and objects: the old Sumerians used incipits to form surrogate summaries, which they could browse, while later document titles were invented and are still the most important form of metadata. Library cards such as the one in Figure 2.1 have for centuries recorded metadata such as title, author, year of publication, classification tag, location in library, publisher with their address, and so on.

```
     Multimedia Information Retrieval / Stefan Rüger


IR223.34.K26 Rueger, Stefan
R18          San Rafael, Calif.:
2010         Morgan & Claypool Publ., 2010
               iv, 155p, 73 ill., 4 vid., 1 soundf.
             ISBN paper 9781608450978
             ISBN ebook 9781608450985
```

Figure 2.1: What library cards looked like

The printed out library card has become obsolete, and the most important technique for multimedia retrieval based on metadata has become structured-document retrieval. Document structure is increasingly often expressed in the XML schema language[1] of the World Wide Web Consortium[2]. Lalmas (2009) covers XML Retrieval in depth.

When using metadata, it becomes apparent how vital it is that they can be exchanged, especially so in digital libraries. One of the oldest and most widespread standards for bibliographic metadata is MARC, which stands for machine-readable cataloguing. It is an elaborate standard with several hundred entries that are subject to the Anglo-American Cataloguing Rules in its current version AARC2R. Owing to the complexity of these rules, only trained specialists are able to create a MARC record. However, once created, a record can then be shared by libraries all over the world. It is the use of standards such as MARC that have made it possible to create and search the Worldcat union catalogue at OCLC of currently more than 150 million entries in 470 languages[3]. MARCXML is the corresponding XML language that expresses a MARC record in XML.

---

[1]http://www.w3.org/XML/Schema
[2]http://www.w3.org
[3]http://www.oclc.org/worldcat/statistics/charts/languagecloud.htm as of Nov 2009

On the other side of the spectrum of complexity resides the Dublin Core standard named after the city in Ohio, US, where the first meeting took place in 1995. Its almost trivial structure — only 15 elements such as title, creator, subject, description and date each of which is optional and may be repeated — make it very easy for everyone to instantly create metadata for their multimedia objects. The Dublin Core metadata initiative have produced a comprehensive and comprehensible guide Using Dublin Core[4]. Figure 2.2 shows an XML representation of simple Dublin Core metadata for this book.

```
<?xml version="1.0"?>
<metadata
    xmlns="http://w.x.y/z/"
    xmlns:xsi="http://www.w3.org/2001/XMLSchema-instance"
    xsi:schemaLocation="http://w.x.y/z/ http://w.x.y/z/schema.xsd"
    xmlns:dc="http://purl.org/dc/elements/1.1/">

    <dc:title> Multimedia information retrieval </dc:title>
    <dc:description>
        This book covers the process of finding multimedia documents, how to
        build multimedia search engines, and guides through related research.
    </dc:description>
    <dc:creator> Stefan Rueger </dc:creator>
    <dc:date> 2010 </dc:date>
    <dc:publisher> San Rafael, Ca: Morgan & Claypool Publishers </dc:publisher>
    <dc:identifier>
        http://dx.doi.org/10.2200/S00224ED1V01Y200910ICR010
    </dc:identifier>
    <dc:identifier> ISBN paper 9781608450978 </dc:identifier>
    <dc:identifier> ISBN ebook 9781608450985 </dc:identifier>
</metadata>
```

Figure 2.2: Dublin core record for this book

Metadata are not always stored outside the documents themselves. Many multimedia documents contain provisions for storing metadata, especially technical metadata. For example, the *tagged image file format* TIFF contains an internal directory structure to hold many images in one file; each image can have its own description in terms of size, bit sampling information, compression and so on. Although all images are rectangular, the format allows for a vector-based cropping path for outlines or image frames. TIFF was initially conceived for scanners but is now a good format for any digital image no matter what the source, be it a screenshot, a digital camera, a grey-level scan, a photo-editing programme or a medical imaging device. The TIFF standard is extensible and some companies have created proprietary image file formats on the back of TIFF describing using custom compression schemes or additional tags. Nikon's NEF format is one such example. Most digital libraries chose to store images in TIFF with lossless compression, which is also the best format to

[4]http://dublincore.org/documents/usageguide

process images in photo-editors — a lossy file format such as JPEG would otherwise lose some of its quality in each store-reload step.

Most camera manufacturers have agreed on a way of incorporating metadata into the files that the camera produces; this is the so-named *exchangeable image file format* EXIF that records mostly technical (as opposed to descriptive) metadata, including a thumbnail of the image, see Figure 2.3 for an example for the kind of information that can be stored in it. EXIF metadata can be stored in TIFF.

Model	Nikon D200
Exposure	Auto exposure, aperture priority, pattern metering
Exposure	1/640, f8.0, +0.78eV, 100 ISO, 15mm focal length
Flash	did not fire
Orientation	top_left
Date	22.07.2007 12.45 BST
GPS data	52 ° 03'27.6"N, 0 ° 43'30.0"W, 71m
Media	3872x2592 image/jpeg Baseline Fine (4:1)
Thumbnail	Bits/channel 8 8 8

Figure 2.3: Some EXIF metadata for a JPEG photograph

Other file formats associate different metadata standards with them. Adobe Systems, for example, pushes its *extensible metadata platform* XMP that is very versatile and includes, amongst other things, rights management. Originally developed for Adobe's Portable Document Format, its structure can be applied to images, audio and video files alike. In 2008 the International Press Telecommunications Council released a photo metadata standard based on XMP. The Library of Congress' Network Development and MARC Standards Office promotes a different XML schema for a set of technical data elements required to manage digital image collections. The schema, also known as *Metadata for Images in XML* (MIX), provides an alternative format for interchange and/or storage.

The most salient metadata standard for multimedia is MPEG-7, which was developed by MPEG (Moving Picture Experts Group)[5] and is a format for description and search of audiovisual resources. MPEG-7 also contains low-level descriptors that can be used with content-based queries. As such, MPEG-7 is the ideal choice of meta-data for audiovisual search engines. MPEG-7 also proposes a set of features that can be used for this purpose, but the standard does not suggest nor prescribe how content-based queries should be carried out. Section 2.3 and Chapter 3 will go into more detail how content-based queries can be processed.

MPEG-7 descriptions cater for still images, graphics, 3d models, audio, speech, video, and information about how these elements are composed in a multimedia presentation. They care about the *content* of the multimedia object on various levels, from low-level machine-extractable features,

---

[5] Other MPEG standards include MPEG-1 and MPEG-2, which enabled video on CD-ROM, MP3, Digital Audio Broadcasting and Digital Television through compression; MPEG-4, which is the multimedia standard to support animation and interactivity; MPEG 21, which is a metadata standard for content delivery and rights management

to high-level human annotations, but they do *not* engage with the way the content is represented: physical world objects such as a drawing on paper can have an MPEG-7 description in the very same way as a compressed digital TIFF image.

As with other metadata standards, there is not a single one "right" MPEG-7 file for a particular multimedia object. MPEG-7 allows, and encourages, different levels of granularity in the description depending on the application type. Although MPEG-7 puts a great emphasis on content description, more traditional metadata such as media type, rights information, price and parental ratings can also be included. The three main elements of MPEG-7 are:

- *Descriptors* to define the syntax and the semantics of each feature, and *description schemes* to specify the relationships between their components, which in turn may be descriptors and description schemes

- *Description definition language* to define the syntax of the MPEG-7 description tools and to allow the creation of new description schemes and descriptors

- *System tools and reference implementations* to support binary coded representation for efficient storage and transmission, multiplexing of descriptions, synchronization of descriptions with content, management and protection of rights

Figure 2.4 shows an MPEG-7 encoding of the results of an algorithm that predicts the presence of *tree*, *field* and *horses* with various levels of confidence. Can you spot those words? More information about MPEG-7 can be found at the MPEG[6] website and the MPEG-7 Consortium website[7].

Witten et al (2010, Chapter 6) give a deeper insight into metadata in general and their use within digital libraries, but see also (Hillmann and Westbrooks, 2004; Gilliland-Swetland, 1998; Intner et al, 2006; Lagoze and Payette, 2000; Zeng and Qin, 2008; Messing et al, 2001).

2.2   PIGGY-BACK TEXT RETRIEVAL

Amongst all media types, TV video streams arguably have the biggest scope for automatically extracting text strings in a number of ways: directly from closed-captions, teletext or subtitles; automated speech recognition on the audio and optical character recognition for text embedded in the frames of a video. Full text search of these strings is the way in which most video retrieval systems operate, including Google's latest TV search engine[8] or Blinkx-TV[9]. This technology existed in some research labs much earlier: for example, Físchlár-TV[10] was an experimental web-based video recorder system, developed and maintained 1999–2004 by Dublin City University's Centre for Digital Video

---

[6]http://www.chiariglione.org/mpeg
[7]http://mpeg7.nist.gov
[8]http://video.google.com
[9]http://www.blinkx.tv
[10]http://www.cdvp.dcu.ie/aboutfischlar.html

```
<?xml version="1.0" encoding="UTF-8"?>
<Mpeg7 xsi:schemaLocation="urn:mpeg:mpeg7:schema:2004 ./davp-2005.xsd"
xmlns="urn:mpeg:mpeg7:schema:2004"
xmlns:mpeg="urn:mpeg:mpeg7:schema:2004"
xmlns:xsi="http://www.w3.org/2001/XMLSchema-instance">
  <Description xsi:type="ContentEntityType">
    <MultimediaContent xsi:type="AudioVisualType">
      <AudioVisual>
        <StructuralUnit href="urn:x-mpeg-7-pharos:cs:AudioVisualSegmentationCS:root"/>
        <MediaSourceDecomposition criteria="kmi image annotation segment">
          <StillRegion>
            <MediaLocator>
              <MediaUri>http://server/location/Zion_National_Park_392099.jpg</MediaUri>
            </MediaLocator>
            <StructuralUnit href="urn:x-mpeg-7-pharos:cs:SegmentationCS:image"/>
            <TextAnnotation type="urn:x-mpeg-7-pharos:cs:TextAnnotationCS:
                image:keyword:kmi:annotation_1" confidence="0.87">
              <FreeTextAnnotation>tree</FreeTextAnnotation>
            </TextAnnotation>
            <TextAnnotation type="urn:x-mpeg-7-pharos:cs:TextAnnotationCS:
                image:keyword:kmi:annotation_2" confidence="0.72">
              <FreeTextAnnotation>field</FreeTextAnnotation>
            </TextAnnotation>
            <TextAnnotation type="urn:x-mpeg-7-pharos:cs:TextAnnotationCS:
                image:keyword:kmi:annotation_3" confidence="0.63">
              <FreeTextAnnotation>horses</FreeTextAnnotation>
            </TextAnnotation>
          </StillRegion>
        </MediaSourceDecomposition>
      </AudioVisual>
    </MultimediaContent>
  </Description>
</Mpeg7>
```

Figure 2.4: MPEG-7 example for automated text annotation of an image

Processing. A final-year student project at Imperial College London that indexed videos through teletext received a national prize in the year 2000[11], see also Section 4.1.

In contrast to television, for which legislation normally requires subtitles to assist the hearing impaired, videos stored on DVD don't usually have textual subtitles. They have *subpicture* channels for different languages instead, which are overlaid on the video stream. This requires the extra step of optical character recognition, which can be done with a relatively low error rate owing to good quality fonts and clear background/foreground separation in the subpictures. In general, teletext has a much lower word error rate than automated speech recognition. In practice, it turns out that

[11]http://www.setawards.org/previous_winners.vc

this does not matter too much as query words often occur repeatedly in the audio - the retrieval performance degrades gracefully with increased word error rates.

Web pages afford some context information that can be used for indexing multimedia objects. For example, words in the anchor text of a link to an image, a video clip or a music track, the file name of the object itself, metadata stored within the files and other context information such as captions. A subset of these sources for text snippets are normally used in web image search engines.

Some symbolic music representations allow the conversion of music into text, such as MIDI files which contain a music representation in terms of pitch, onset times and duration of notes. By representing differences of successive pitches as characters one can, for example, map monophonic music to one-dimensional strings as demonstrated in Figure 2.5. The numbers are midi representations of the pitch of the score. We just record the differences of successive notes (as only a few gifted ones have the power of absolute pitch) and convert the difference to a letter. Zero is Z, 1 is upper case *A*, -1 is lowercase *a*, and so on. The process in Figure 2.5 glides a window over the music piece and records "musical words" of a certain length. These words then act as surrogate text for music representation; query by humming can thus be treated as a text retrieval problem. Downie and Nelson (2000) were the first to map music to text in this way. Later Doraisamy (2005) deployed this principle and extended it to both polyphonic music, where more than one note is present, and rhythm, ie, music retrieval by tapping. She built a query by humming system that is based on the reduction of music to text followed by text search: you can watch a demonstration video that lays open the individual steps of her algorithm by clicking on Figure 2.5 or by going directly to http://people.kmi.open.ac.uk/stefan/mir-book/movie0008-audio.wmv.

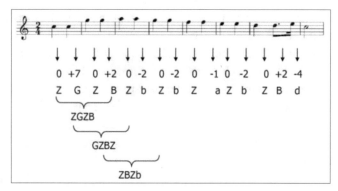

Figure 2.5: Music Retrieval by Humming (click frame to play demo video)

A large range of different text matching techniques can be deployed, for example, the edit distance of database strings with a string representation of a query. The edit distance between two strings computes the smallest number of deletions, insertions or character replacements that is necessary to transform one string into the other. In the case of query-by-humming, where a pitch tracker can convert the hummed query into a MIDI-sequence (Birmingham et al, 2006), the edit distance is also able to deal gracefully with humming errors.

2.3   CONTENT-BASED RETRIEVAL

Content-based retrieval uses characteristics of the multimedia objects themselves, ie, their content to search and find multimedia. Its main application is to find multimedia by examples, ie, when the query consists not of words but of a similar example instance.

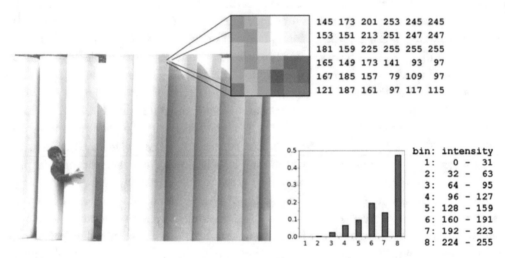

Figure 2.6: Millions of pixels with intensity values and the corresponding intensity histogram

One of the difficulties of matching multimedia is that the parts the media are made from are not necessarily semantic units. Another difficulty comes about by the sheer amount of data with little apparent structure. Look at the black and white photograph of Figure 2.6, for example. It literally consists of millions of pixels, and each of the pixels encodes an intensity (one number between 0=black and 255=white) or a colour (three numbers for the red, green and blue colour channel, say). One of the prime tasks in multimedia retrieval is to make sense out of this sea of numbers.

The key here is to condense the sheer amount of numbers into meaningful pieces of information, which we call *features*. One trivial example is to compute an intensity histogram, ie, count which proportion of the pixels falls into which intensity ranges. In Figure 2.6 I have chosen 8 ranges, and the histogram of 8 numbers conveys a rough distribution of brightness in the image.

Figure 2.7 shows the main principle of *query-by-example*; in this case, the query is the image of an ice-bear on the left. This query image will have a representation as a certain point (o) in feature space. In the same way, every single image in the database has its own representation (x) in the same space. The images, whose representations are closest to the representation of the query are ranked top by this process. The two key elements really are features and distances. Our choice of feature space and how to compute distances has a vital impact on how well visual search by example works.

Features and distances are a vital part of content-based retrieval and so is the ability to efficiently find nearest neighbours in high-dimensional spaces. This is the content of Chapter 3

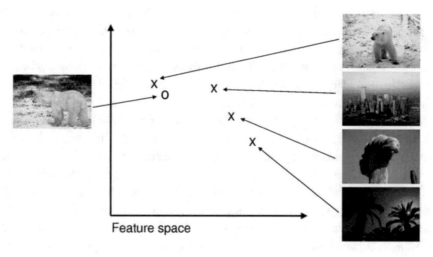

Figure 2.7: Features and distances

that treats content-based retrieval in depth. Lew et al (2006) and Datta et al (2008) have published overview articles on content-based retrieval.

2.4   AUTOMATED IMAGE ANNOTATION

Two of the factors limiting the uptake of digital libraries for multimedia are the scarcity and the expense of metadata for digital media. Flickr[12], a popular photo sharing site, lets users upload, organise and annotate their own photographs with tags. In order to search images in Flickr, little more than user tags are available with the effect that many photographs are difficult or impossible to find. The same is true for the video sharing site YouTube[13]. At the other end of the spectrum are commercial sites such as the digital multimedia store iTunes[14], which sells music, movies, TV shows, audio-books, podcasts and games. They tend to have sufficiently many annotations as the commercial nature of iTunes makes it viable to supply metadata to the required level of granularity. While personal photographs and videos do not come with much metadata except for the data that the camera provides (time-stamp and technical data such as aperture, exposure, sensitivity and focal length), a whole class of surveillance data carries even less incentive to create metadata manually: CCTV recordings, satellite images, audio recordings in the sea and other sensor data. The absence of labels and metadata is a real barrier for complex and high-level queries such as "what did the person with a red jumper look like who exited the car park during the last 6 hours in a black Volvo at high speed".

[12]http://flickr.com
[13]http://www.youtube.com
[14]http://www.apple.com/itunes

One way to generate useful tags and metadata for multimedia objects is to involve a community of people who do the tagging collaboratively. This process is also called folksonomy, social indexing or social tagging. Del.icio.us[15] is a social bookmarking system and a good example for folksonomies. Similarly, the ability of Flickr to annotate images of other people falls also into this category. Von Ahn and Dabbish (2004) have invented a computer game that provides an incentive (competition and points) for people to label randomly selected images. All these approaches tap into "human computing power" for a good cause: the structuring and labelling of multimedia objects. Research in this area is still in the beginning, and it is by no way clear how to best harness the social power of collaborative tagging to improve metadata for, and access to, digital museums and libraries.

Another way to bridge the semantic gap (see Figure 1.7) is to try to assign simple words automatically to images solely based on their pixels. Methods attempting this task include dedicated machine vision models for particular words such as "people" or "aeroplane". These individual models for each of the words can quickly become very detailed and elaborate: Thomas Huang of the University of Illinois at Urbana Champaign once joked during his keynote speech at CIVR 2002 that in order to enable a system to annotate 1,000 words automatically, it was merely a case of supervising 1,000 corresponding PhD projects!

Automated annotation can be formulated in more general terms of machine translation as seen in Figure 2.8. The basic idea is to first dissect images into blobs of similar colour and then use these blobs as "words" of a visual vocabulary. Given a training set of annotated images a correlation between certain words and certain blobs can then be established in a similar way to correlations between corresponding words of two different languages using a parallel corpus (for example, the official records of the Canadian Parliament in French and English). Duygulu et al (2002) created the first successful automated annotation mechanisms based on this idea.

Figure 2.8: Automated annotation as machine translation problem

However, the most popular and successful *generic* approaches are based on classification techniques. This normally requires a large training set of images that have annotations from which one can extract features and correlate these with the existing annotations of the training set. For ex-

---

[15]http://del.icio.us

ample, images with tigers will have orange-black stripes and often green patches from surrounding vegetation, and their existence in an unseen image can in turn bring about the annotation "tiger". As with any machine learning method, it is important to work with a large set of training examples. Figure 2.9 shows randomly selected, royalty free images from the Corel's Gallery 380,000 product that were annotated with *sunset* (top) and *city* (bottom). Each of these images can have multiple annotations: there are pictures that are annotated with *both* sunset and city, and possibly other terms.

Automated algorithms build a model for the commonalities in the features of images, which can later be used for retrieval. One of the simplest machine learning algorithms is the Naïve Bayes formula,

$$P(w|i) = \frac{P(w, i)}{P(i)} = \frac{\sum_j P(w, i|j)P(j)}{\sum_j P(i|j)P(j)}$$

$$= \frac{\sum_j P(i|w, j)P(w|j)P(j)}{\sum_j \sum_w P(i|w, j)P(w|j)P(j)},$$

where j are training images, w are word annotations and $P(w|i)$ is the probability of a word w given an (unseen) image i. The probability $P(w, j)$ that word w is used to annotate image j can be estimated from an empirical distribution of annotations in the training data.

Figure 2.10 shows an unseen image i for which the five words with the highest probabilities $p(w|i)$ according to above Naïve Bayes classification are all sensible and useful.

Yavlinsky et al (2005) built models based on a similar idea for which the model for keywords appearance is derived from non-parametric density estimators with specialised kernels that utilise the Earth mover's distance. The assumption is that these kernels reflect the nature of the underlying features well. Yavlinsky built a corresponding search engine behold[16], where one could search for Flickr images using these detected terms. These algorithms all make errors as one can expect from fully automated systems. Figure 2.11 shows screenshots from an early version of behold. Clearly, not all words are predicted correctly, and the ugly examples from this figure might motivate to study methods that use external knowledge, for example, that stairs and icebergs normally do not go together.

Today, Makadia et al's recent (2008) work on the nearest neighbour label transfer provide a baseline for automatic image annotation using global low-level features and a straightforward label transfer from the 5 nearest neighbours. This approach is likely to work very well if enough images are available in a labelled set that are very close to the unlabelled application set. This may be the case, for example, in museums where images of groups of objects are taken in a batch fashion with the same lighting and background and only some of the objects in the group have received manual labels. Liu et al (2009a) also use label transfer, albeit in a slightly different setting since they aim to segment and recognise scenes rather than assign global classification labels.

---

[16]http://www.behold.cc

Figure 2.9: Machine learning training samples for *sunset* (top) and *city* images (bottom)

Figure 2.10: Automated annotation results in *water*, *buildings*, *city*, *sunset* and *aerial*

Automated annotation from pixels faces criticism not only owing to its current inability to model a large and useful vocabulary with high accuracy. Enser and Sandom (2002, 2003) argue that some of the vital information for significance and content of images *has* to come from metadata: it is virtually impossible to, eg, compute the date or location of an image from its pixels. A real-world image query such as "Stirling Moss winning Kentish 100 Trophy at Brands Hatch, 30 August 1968" cannot be answered without metadata. They argue that pixel-based algorithms will never be able to compute *significance* of images such as "first public engagement of Prince Charles as a boy" or "the first ordination of a woman as bishop". Their UK-funded arts and humanities research project "Bridging the Semantic Gap in Visual Information Retrieval" (Hare et al, 2006; Enser and Sandom, 2003) brought a new understanding about the role of the semantic gap in visual image retrieval.

Owing to these observations and also owing to their relatively large error rates, automated annotation methods seem to be more suitable in the context of browsing or in conjunction with other search methods. For example, if you want to "find shots of the front of the White House in the daytime with the fountain running"[17], then a query-by-example search in a large database may be solved quicker and better by emphasising those shots that were classified as "vegetation", "outside", "building" etc — even though the individual classification may be wrong in a significant proportion of cases.

There is a host of research that supports the bridging of the semantic gap via automated annotation. Hare and Lewis (2004) use salient interest points and the concept of scale to the selection of salient regions in an image to describe the image characteristics in that region; they then extended this work (2005) to model visual terms from a training set that can then be used to annotate unseen images. Magalhães and Rüger (2006) developed a clustering method that is more computationally efficient than the currently very effective method of non-parametric density estimation, which they later (2007) integrated into a unique multimedia indexing model for heterogeneous data. Torralba and Oliva (2003) obtained relatively good results with simple scene-level statistics,

[17]Topic 124 of TRECVid 2003, see http://www-nlpir.nist.gov/projects/tv2003

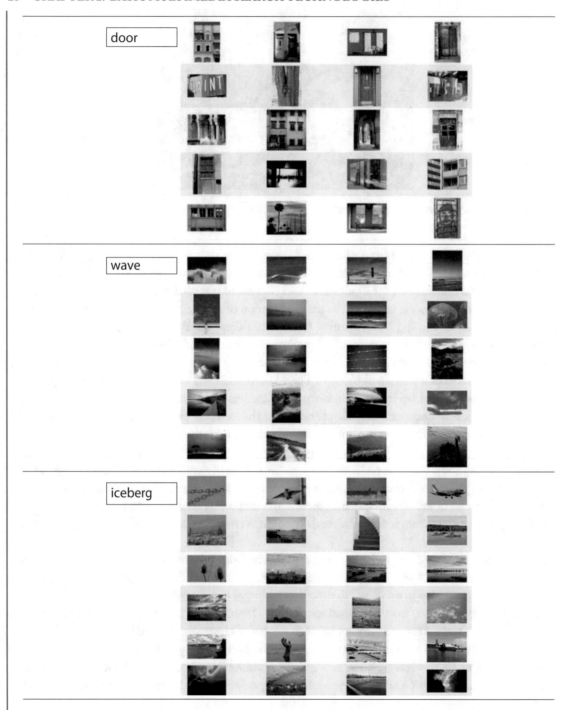

Figure 2.11: The good, the bad and the ugly: three examples for automated annotation

while others deploy more complex models: Jeon et al (2003) and Lavrenko et al (2003) studied cross-lingual information retrieval models, while Metzler and Manmatha (2004) set up inference networks that connect image segments with words. Blei and Jordan (2003) carry out probabilistic modelling with latent Dirichlet allocation, while Feng et al (2004) use Bernoulli distributions.

Machine learning methods for classification and annotation are not limited to images at all. For example, one can extract motion vectors from MPEG-encoded videos and use these to classify a video shot independently into categories such as object motion from left to right, zoom in, tilt, roll, dolly in and out, truck left and right, pedestal up and down, crane boom, swing boom etc. In contrast to the above classification tasks, the extracted motion vector features are much more closely correlated to the ensuing motion label than image features are to text labels, and the corresponding learning task should be much simpler a consequence.

The application area for classification can be rather diverse: Baillie and Jose (2004) use audio analysis of the crowd response in a football game to detect important events in the match; Cavallaro and Ebrahimi (2004) propose an interaction mechanism between the semantic and the region partitions, which allows to detect multiple simultaneous objects in videos.

On a higher level, Salway and Graham (2003) developed a method to extract information about emotions of characters in films and suggested that this information can help describe higher levels of multimedia semantics relating to narrative structures. Salway et al (2005) contributed to the analysis and description of semantic video content by investigating what actions are important in films.

Musical genre classification can be carried out on extracted audio-features that represent a performance by its statistics of pitch content, rhythmic structure and timbre texture (Tzanetakis and Cook, 2002): timbre texture features are normally computed using short-time Fourier transform and Mel-frequency cepstral coefficients that also play a vital role in speech recognition; the rhythmic structure of music can be explored using discrete wavelet transforms that have a different time resolution for different frequencies; pitch detection, especially in polyphonic music, is more intricate and requires more elaborate algorithms. For details, see the work of Tolonen and Karjalainen (2000). Tzanetakis and Cook (2002) report correct classification rates of between 40% (rock) and 75% (jazz) in their experiments with 10 different genres.

2.5   FINGERPRINTING

Multimedia fingerprints are a means to uniquely identify multimedia objects in a database, given a possibly different representation of it. Fingerprints are computed from the contents of the multimedia objects. They are small, allow the fast, reliable and *unique* location of the database record and, most importantly, are robust against degradation or deliberate change as long as the *human perception* is the same.

The idea is to be able to identify a specific multimedia object based solely on its content. For example, you listen to a song in a restaurant and would like to know more about it. You could record a piece of the song and use this representation to query a database of performances. Your recording will be degraded by background noise, and it will be only a part of the original performance. Its fingerprint should be sufficient to uniquely determine the entry in your large database of original recordings, say, CD tracks as published by the music industry. This does not mean that the fingerprint of the query has to be identical to the fingerprint of the original multimedia object — the former needs only contain enough evidence to identify the original fingerprint beyond reasonable doubt. This also means that we would expect to distinguish even between different performances of the same song by the same artist at different occasions. Sinitsyn (2006) explains how audio fingerprinting algorithms can be integrated into data management middleware to perform background self-cleaning from duplicates.

Fingerprinting is just as useful in the visual world: for example, consider videos uploaded to YouTube, a video sharing site. The uploaded video may already exist in YouTube, but have been transcoded for a different bandwidth into a different format, edited to conform to a different aspect ratio, may have logos or advertisement inserted, but its fingerprint should still identify it as a copy of another one already in the database.

As we want to identify objects based on perception, simple hashes such as Message Digest algorithm 5 (MD5) or the Cyclic Redundancy Check (CRC) of the multimedia contents are not sufficient: these would already change when a single bit of the file is changed, let alone when the whole representation and encoding of the multimedia object radically changed.

2.5.1   AUDIO FINGERPRINTING

For audio, many fingerprinting algorithms are based on the spectrogram of the song. A spectrogram is a threeway graph telling us which frequencies contain how much energy at which time of the audio piece. Salient points of a spectrogram are time-frequency points (τ, f) that contain a relatively high amount of energy. In order to compute the energy as a function of the frequency at a given point τ in time, the original pressure-wave sound signal $\tau \mapsto s(\tau)$ is subjected to a short window around τ in time. Rather than using rectangular windows that would harshly cut off the signal and artificially introduce high frequencies near the cut-off points, one uses smooth infinite windows such as a Gaussian or, more popularly, a finite Hann window $t \mapsto w(t) = (1 - \cos(2\pi(t - \tau)/T))/2$ with width T on the interval $[\tau - T/2, \tau + T/2]$. This short-term signal is then subjected to a Fourier transform, the magnitude of which is known as the energy distribution in frequency space:

$$\text{spectrogram}(f, \tau) = \left| \int_{-\infty}^{\infty} s(t)w(t - \tau)e^{jft}dt \right|^2$$

In practice, the spectrogram is computed as the squared modulus of the discrete short-term Fourier transform using discrete time and frequency variables and sums instead of integrals.

Other transformations are in use, such as the Modulated complex lapped transform, the Walsh-Hadamard transform or variants of the Fourier transform, from all of which robust features are extracted (Cano et al, 2005). In the following few paragraphs, we will look at two detailed mechanisms to find known pieces of music in a database from spectrograms: Shazam's constellation maps (Wang, 2003) and Philips Research's fingerprint blocks (Haitsma and Kalker, 2003). Shazam[18] actually provides a service that allows you to capture snippets of music via your mobile phone and returns one of the 8 million tracks in their database[19].

Figure 2.12 is a screenshot of audacity, a free digital audio editor, displaying a spectrogram of a 5 second light sabre sound from Star Wars. The bright points in the colour spectrogram correspond to the peaks in the energy. The important point to remember is that the location of these peaks would remain invariant under varying compression, audio encoding, background noise etc. The light sabre sound has a characteristic near continuous band of high energy in the low frequencies in addition to columns of energy spread over the whole frequency spectrum. Once quantised with a suitable algorithm, we get distinct salient points in the spectrum, see Figure 2.13. In music pieces, they look a bit like star constellations, which is why Wang (2003) has called the scatter plot of these points *constellation maps*.

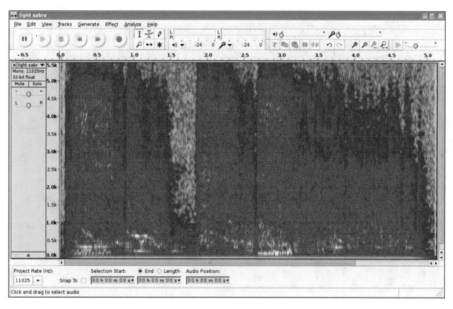

Figure 2.12: Audacity screenshot of the spectrogram of a light sabre sound

The quantised coordinate list for the constellation maps recording peak energy is sparse and discrete. The problem of detecting the song in the database is reduced to a registration problem of the constellation maps: Imagine the constellation maps of all database songs on a long strip of paper and the query's constellation map on a small piece of transparency foil. You find the matching music piece by gliding the transparency over the paper strip and noting the best match.

---

[18]http://www.shazam.com
[19]http://www.shazam.com/music/web/newsdetail.html?nid=NEWS103 (last accessed Apr 2009)

Wang (2003) used certain *pairs* of constellation points to search for matches: for each constellation point (also called anchor point) he considers a fixed rectangular target zone to the right of the anchor point and uses all pairs that consist of the anchor point and a point in target zone. Each of these constellation pairs is encoded as its pair of frequencies and the time difference making the representation time invariant. With a suitable discretisation of the time and frequency axis, say 10 bits each, these three values can be packed into a 32-bit hash value that associates the song id and time offset of the anchor point within the song to it, see Figure 2.13. The use of constellation pairs instead of points increases the specificity of a single match of a constellation pair (as opposed to a point) by a factor of $2^{20} \approx 1,000,000$ (30 bits vs 10 bits). Let us assume that the dimension of the target zone is constructed in a way that the number of constellation points in it is limited to, on average, n points, say $n = 10$. Then there are n times more pairs to store than there are points and there are n times more query pairs to match than there are anchor points. This reduces the speed-up factor of one match to approximately $1,000,000/n^2 = 10,000$, assuming $n = 10$.

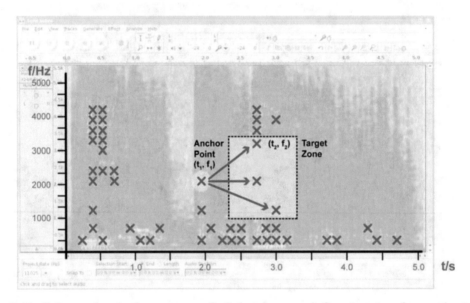

Figure 2.13: Salient points in the spectrum of a light sabre sound. Certain pairs of spectral points are used for retrieval and encoded as as the hash function $(f_1, f_2, t_2 - t_1) \mapsto (t_1, id)$. The visualised salient points here are not to scale: see Exercise 2.6.5.

The actual matching process is straightforward: the audio query, which is a captured part of a song, is processed and hash values of certain constellation pairs (as described above) are extracted. Each of the hashes is looked up in the database of constellation pairs hashes of all songs. Each match results in three pieces of information: the time t_1^q of the anchor point in the query hash, the time t_1^d of the matching anchor point in the database and the corresponding song id. For a true match of the music sample with a particular song, the matched pairs need to align consistently in time. As the query only captures a part of the song, which can start anywhere in the song, the times of the anchor points of query and matching song will not be the same, but their difference $t_1^d - t_1^q$ is expected to be a constant for true matches, and this constant should be the starting time of the captured query in the full song. Separating true matches from spurious ones can thus be done with the following method: for each song, in which a match of a constellation pair occurred, keep a small histogram of the observed differences $t_1^d - t_1^q$. One of these histograms is expected to exhibit a substantial peak in a particular time difference, and the corresponding song will be the right one from the database.

Haitsma and Kalker (2003) from Philips Research suggest to use the spectrogram for their fingerprints, too. They extract a 32-bit sub-fingerprint every 11.6 ms (the granularity of the time axis) and collect 256 adjacent sub-fingerprints into a block covering around 3 s of music. They divide the frequency scale between 300 Hz and 2,000 Hz into 33 logarithmically spaced frequency bands, so that the distance between two neighbouring frequency bands becomes roughly 1/12 of an octave, or a semitone. Let $E(m, n)$ denote the energy of the mth frequency band at the nth time frame of 11.6 ms. Then the mth bit of the nth frame is set to the sign of the following neighbouring energy differences ($0 \leq m \leq 31$ and $0 \leq n \leq 255$):

$$[E(m, n) - E(m + 1, n)] - [E(m, n + 1) - E(m + 1, n + 1)] \tag{2.1}$$

They argue that the sign of this energy difference is relatively robust under different encoding schemes. A partial fingerprint block for the light sabre sound is depicted in Fig 2.14. In theory this is now a similar registration and matching problem as in Shazam's representation, but it is approached differently here. The reason for this is presumably owing to the fact that perceptually same music pieces can exhibit a bit error rate of 10-30% between matching fingerprint blocks. Indeed, Haitsma and Kalker (2003) set a threshold of 35%: if the bit error rate between two fingerprint blocks falls below 35% then they declare these two blocks as coming from the same song.

Even though a high bit error rate of $b = 0.3$ causes the probability $p(4)$ that no more than 4 bits were flipped to drop under 2%, it is the case that when you look at 256 sub-fingerprints, at least one of them will have no more than 4 bit errors with more than 99% probability (see Exercise 2.6.3).

The basic search idea is to go through the 256 sub-fingerprints in a query block and try to match each sub-fingerprint against a database sub-fingerprint. If there is a match of two sub-fingerprints, then the corresponding blocks are compared; if, furthermore, the bit error rate is below the threshold, then a match is declared on the corresponding song. If no matching song was found when checking all 256 sub-fingerprints in the query, then it is assumed that none of the 256 sub-fingerprints of the query has survived the transformation from the original song unscathed. The next best thing is to assume that at least one of the query sub-fingerprints has only one bit flipped. This gives rise to 32 different sub-fingerprints with one changed bit. If the next round of checks with $256 \cdot 32$ modified sub-fingerprints from the query does not identify a matching song then 2 bit-errors are assumed to have happened in the query. There would be $\binom{32}{2} = 32 \cdot 31/2 = 496$ different combinations that can be produced from each sub-fingerprint. As this is getting more and more computationally expensive, Haitsma and Kalker (2003) suggest a heuristics: they assume that bits in the query sub-fingerprints are more susceptible to bit changes if they arise from energy differences (2.1) closer to zero. They would only create modified query sub-fingerprints for the most susceptible bits. This makes it feasible to explore variations where more than 2 bits are changed. If after all reasonable attempts still no matching block could be identified, it is assumed that the query song was either too distorted or is not in the database.

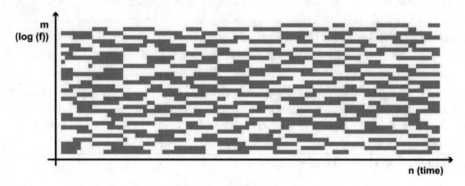

Figure 2.14: Partial fingerprint block of initial light sabre sound

Audio fingerprints of music tracks are expected to distinguish even between different performances of the same song by the same artist at different occasions.

Interesting applications include services that allow broadcast monitoring companies to identify what was played, so that royalties are fairly distributed or programmes and advertisements verified. Other applications uncover copyright violation or, for example, provide a service that allows you to locate the metadata such as title, artist and date of performance from snippets recorded on a (noisy) mobile phone.

2.5.2   IMAGE FINGERPRINTING

The requirements for image fingerprints are the same as for audio fingerprints: they should be small, and allow the fast, reliable and *unique* location of the database record under degradation or small deliberate change. The main difference between Images and Audio is that images are static two-dimensional colour distributions, while sound is a one-dimensional air pressure function of time. We will look at different ways to record image features, so that similar images can be recognised "beyond a reasonable doubt". The underlying basic idea is to create a number L of *independent* representations, each of which maps near duplicates to the same quantised value with a reasonable, but not necessarily very high probability; this quantised value corresponds to the constellation pair hash for audio fingerprinting. The next step is to require a match of a certain number m out of the L independent representations between two images for them to be declared near identical. In the following, we will look at one method, locality sensitive hashing (LSH), for near-duplicate detection for dense features and one, min hash, for sparse features.[20]

Locality Sensitive Hashing

LSH (Datar et al, 2004) consists of independent random projections of the original feature space to integers that are combined into a hash value. The basic procedure maps a feature vector $v \in \mathbb{R}^d$ to an integer

$$h^i(v) = \left\lfloor \frac{a^i v + b^i}{w} \right\rfloor, \qquad (2.2)$$

where $a^i \in \mathbb{R}^d$ is a random vector with independent normal distributed components, $w \in \mathbb{R}^+$ is a constant specifying the granularity of the results and $b^i \in [0, w)$ is a random uniformly distributed number. A k-tuple of these integers defines a composite hash-value

$$h(v) = (h^1(v), h(^2(v), \ldots, h^k(v)).$$

The preimage in feature space of a particular hash-value is an area that is bordered by pairs of hyperplanes that are perpendicular to one of the random vectors a^i and that have a distance of w. Normally we have $k < d$, which means that the preimage is not bounded. Figure 2.15 visualises how such a hash function works for $k = 2$. Consequently, we have two random vectors $a^1, a^2 \in \mathbb{R}^d$ that determine the orientation of the $d - 1$-dimensional hyperplanes in feature space where the value of the hash function changes. In the figure, each random vector a^i and the corresponding perpendicular hyperplanes are shown in the same colour. The random offsets $b^1, b^2 \in [0, w)$ effectively shift the point of origin in feature space by less than the width w of a hash bin, and they are not visualised here. From the illustration it is clear that nearby points in feature space are likely to end up with the same hash value, though they could have neighbouring hash values owing to boundary effects. It is also apparent that points far away may share the same hash bin. Hence, a series of L independent hash functions is computed for the query with the condition that at least m of these L composite hash values coincide with the corresponding one of a multimedia object before the latter is assumed to be close to the query beyond reasonable doubt.

In practice, only a finite number of bits will be used to store a particular hash integer computed from (2.2). In the example of Figure 2.15, we have 3 bit per axis yielding 6 finite bins and two infinite bins per axis. This setup is only reasonable if we can assume that the points in feature are concentrated on a finite domain (ie, the features are essentially normalised). The composite hash value $h(v)$ only has 6 bit in our example. Note that a reasonable number of bits in a large repository would be around 20 bit, so that a single hash lookup has the potential to reduce the number of points in feature space by a factor of roughly one million (ie, 2^{20}). Based on this the approximate speedup factor should be $L/1,000,000$, as executing a single query means to compute L composite hash values and looking

---

[20]Dense features are ones that are likely to have non-zero components in a fair number of them for a typical image. This would be the case for colour histograms of images. In contrast to this, sparse feature vectors are those for which the number of non-zero components is small, eg, a 'bag of word' representation of text documents or an artificial visual vocabulary for images.

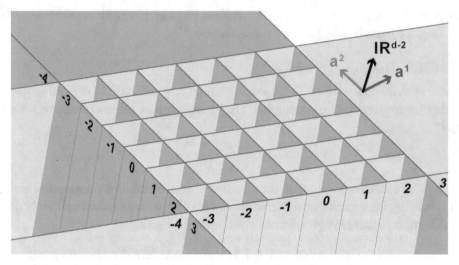

Figure 2.15: Preimage of an LSH function $v \mapsto h(v) = (h^1(v), h^2(v))$ leaving $d-2$ dimensions unbounded in the d-dimensional feature space

up the contents of corresponding, possibly unbounded, hash bins. Those database elements that appear in at least m of the L bins are candidates for nearest neighbours. If precision is important, then the true distance to the query in feature space can be checked for each candidate, but in some applications one might even consider not looking at the feature values of the database elements at all during query time.

Note that w, k and L have to be chosen at index time (unlike m that can be chosen at query time), and their choice should reflect the properties of the repository data in feature space: the product mk ought to exceed d in order for LSH to have a chance of bounding a finite area around the query, while w and k should be chosen so that the typical bin has the desired occupancy.

It looks as if each query can be done in constant time, but — like all hashing techniques — LSH has a query time that is proportional to the number of database entries as the average bucket occupancy increases with the database size. A careful redesign of the hash parameters k and w, however, can reduce the average bucket occupancy once the response is deemed too slow. Although each composite hash value may use only a small disk space, the fact that L hash tables need to be stored makes LSH space-hungry. Ideally, the hash tables are kept in main memory, which limits the number of multimedia entries that can be managed by one single server. In order to alleviate that effectively, kL individual hash values are kept for each feature vector of a multimedia object, one can reuse hash functions: rather than deploying kL random vectors a^i and offsets b^i, one can generate a smaller number n ($2k < n < kL$) of these and randomly chose k out of n vectors and offsets for each of the L composite hash functions. The effect of this reuse is that the composite hash values are not completely independent of each other, but this ultimately saves space.

The significance of using random vectors a^i with components drawn independently from a normal (Gaussian) distribution lies in the fact that their random projections approximately preserve Euclidean distances. It has been argued that Manhattan distances often work better for feature comparisons in content-based image retrieval (Howarth and Rüger, 2005a); random vectors whose components are independently drawn from a particular distribution of family of Cauchy distributions $x \mapsto \frac{c}{\pi} \left(c^2 + x^2\right)^{-1}$ with parameter $c > 0$, approximate Manhattan distances.

Min Hash

Some of the features developed for describing images are sparse, for example, quantised SIFT features from salient image regions. These quantised features share some of the properties of words in language and, hence, are called *visual words*. Let V be the vocabulary of visual words and $A_i \subset V$ be a set of words that describes a particular image i. The similarity between two images i and j can then be expressed as the ratio of the size of the intersection and the union of the representing sets,

$$\text{sim}(A_i, A_j) = \frac{|A_i \cap A_j|}{|A_i \cup A_j|}, \tag{2.3}$$

which is a number between 0 meaning no overlap and 1 meaning identical representing sets. Broder (1997) called this similarity the *resemblance* of two documents and published a method of estimating $\text{sim}(A_i, A_j)$ using random permutations. I will exemplify Broder's algorithm in a simplified form using the following four small text documents:

1. Humpty Dumpty sat on a wall,

2. Humpty Dumpty had a great fall.

3. All the King's horses, And all the King's men

4. Couldn't put Humpty together again!

Removing stop words and putting the words into sets leaves the following four sets:
$A_1 = \{\text{humpty, dumpty, sat, wall}\}$
$A_2 = \{\text{humpty, dumpty, great, fall}\}$
$A_3 = \{\text{all, king, horse, men}\}$
$A_4 = \{\text{put, humpty, together, again}\}$
Equivalently, a document-word matrix of zeros and ones records membership of words in documents. This results in long document vectors, the columns of this matrix:

	A_1	A_2	A_3	A_4
humpty	1	1	0	1
dumpty	1	1	0	0
sat	1	0	0	0
wall	1	0	0	0
great	0	1	0	0
fall	0	1	0	0
all	0	0	1	0
king	0	0	1	0
horse	0	0	1	0
men	0	0	1	0
put	0	0	0	1
together	0	0	0	1
again	0	0	0	1

Using the full document-word matrix for a large collection to compute the inter-document similarities (2.3) is very slow. Owing to the sparsity of the document vectors, the naïve approach of randomly sampling rows of this matrix would result in many uninformative rows for particular documents, ie samples that contain only zeros. Note that for any pair of documents there are only four different rows in the corresponding matrix: (0,0), (0,1), (1,0) and (1,1). It turns out, indeed, that above definition (2.3) of $\text{sim}(A_i, A_j)$ does not depend on how many words occur in neither document: let c_{xy} count the number of (x, y) rows. The key observation is then that

$$\text{sim}(A_i, A_j) = \frac{c_{11}}{c_{11} + c_{10} + c_{01}}, \tag{2.4}$$

ie, $\text{sim}(A_i, A_j)$ is independent of c_{00}. The trick of the min hash is to use a random permutation of the vocabulary, and then, for each document, *only* record its first word under this permutation ignoring all the words that do not occur in the document. This word is called a *min hash*. Consider the following 4 permutations:

$\pi_1 = $ (dumpty, men, again, put, great, humpty, wall, horse, king, sat, fall, together, all)
$\pi_2 = $ (fall, put, all, again, dumpty, sat, men, great, wall, king, horse, humpty, together)
$\pi_3 = $ (horse, dumpty, wall, humpty, great, again, sat, all, men, together, put, king, fall)
$\pi_4 = $ (king, humpty, men, together, great, fall, horse, all, dumpty, wall, sat, again, put)

They give rise to the following min hashes:

	A_1	A_2	A_3	A_4
π_1	dumpty	dumpty	men	again
π_2	dumpty	fall	all	put
π_3	dumpty	dumpty	horse	humpty
π_4	humpty	humpty	king	humpty

The surprising fact is that the probability that the respective min hashes of two documents coincide is equal to $\text{sim}(A_i, A_j)$; this means that $\text{sim}(A_i, A_j)$ can be estimated with a simple counting exercise, namely how often their min hashes coincide under different permutations. In order to understand why this is is the case, let w be the min hash of $A_i \cup A_j$ under a random permutation π, and without restriction of generality, assume $w \in A_i$ implying that w is the min hash of A_i under π. Then w coincides with the min hash of A_j under π if and only if $w \in A_i \cap A_j$. As π is a random permutation, w is chosen from $A_i \cup A_j$ with uniform probability. Consequently, the probability of min hash of A_i coinciding with A_j is exactly the proportion $|A_i \cap A_j|/|A_i \cup A_j|$, ie, $\text{sim}(A_i, A_j)$.

Hence, the proportion of cases where the min hashes of A_i and A_j coincide while π varies is a good approximation of $\text{sim}(A_i, A_j)$ provided the permutations are chosen independently and uniformly. In above example, $\text{sim}(A_1, A_2)$ is estimated to be 3/4 (the true value being 1/2), while $\text{sim}(A_1, A_4)$ is correctly estimated to be 1/4.

Broder (1997) uses the concept of shingles, ie, word sequences in documents, making the representation even more sparse. This is not necessary for image matching as there is no natural order of the visual words in an image. The other generalisation in the original paper is that each min hash records the first s words of a document in the permutation vector.

For the purposes of near duplicate detection k independent min hashes of a document are subsumed into what is called a *sketch*. The probability that two documents have an identical sketch is $\text{sim}(A_i, A_j)^k$. Requiring coinciding sketches reduces the probability of a false positive considerably and will only look at candidates that are highly likely to be very similar. As with LSH, L independent sketches, which act as hash values, are stored for every document. At query time, the sketches of a query document are used to retrieve L sets of documents with the same sketch and the requirement for candidates of near duplicates is to coincide at least m times out of the L sketches.

2.6   EXERCISES

2.6.1   SEARCH TYPES CONTINUED

Coming back to Exercise 1.6.5 and Figure 1.6, what would be the most appropriate search technology (piggy-back text search, feature classification, content-based, fingerprint) for each scenario?

2.6.2   INTENSITY HISTOGRAMS

Revisit Figure 2.6: why is it a good idea to record the *proportion* rather than the absolute value of the number of pixels that fall into the intensity ranges? Explain why these histograms are normalised with respect to the L_1 norm.

2.6.3   FINGERPRINT BLOCK PROBABILITIES

Given a fingerprint block of 256 sub-fingerprints each of which has 32 bits assume the whole block is subjected to an independent identically distributed bit errors at the rate of b. Show that the probability $p(k, b)$ of having no more than k bit errors in one sub-fingerprint is

$$p(k, b) = \sum_{i=0}^{k} \binom{32}{i} (1 - b)^{32-i} b^i.$$

Show that the probability that among 256 sub-fingerprints at least one survives with no more than k bit errors is given by

$$1 - (1 - p(k, b))^{256}.$$

Verify, using above formulas, the following claim on page 31: Even though a high bit error rate of $b = 0.3$ causes the probability $p(4)$ that no more than 4 bits were flipped to drop under 2%, it is the case that when you look at 256 sub-fingerprints, at least one of them will have no more than 4 bit errors with more than 99% probability.

2.6.4   FINGERPRINT BLOCK FALSE POSITIVES

Assuming that the fingerprint block extraction process yields random, independent and identically distributed bits, what is the probability that a randomly modified fingerprint block matches a *different* random block in the database that consists of, say, 10^{11} overlapping fingerprint blocks (4 million songs with around 5 minutes each)? The bit error rate for the random modification is assumed to be 35%.

2.6.5   SHAZAM'S CONSTELLATION PAIRS

Assume that the typical survival probability of each 30-bit constellation pair after deformations that we still want to recognise is p, and that this process is independent per pair. Which encoding density, ie, the number of constellation pairs per second, would you need on average so that a typical captured query of 10 seconds exhibits at least 10 matches in the right song with a probability of at least 99.99%? Under these assumptions, further assuming that the constellation pair extraction looks like a random independent and identically distributed number, what is the false positive rate for a database of 4 million songs each of which is 5 minutes long on average?

2.6.6   ONE PASS ALGORITHM FOR MIN HASH

Rather than actually permuting the rows of the document-word matrix, one would create kL permutation functions $\pi_l : \{1, \ldots, n\} \to \{1, \ldots, n\}, l \in \{1, \ldots, kL\}$, where n is the size of the visual vocabulary (ie, the number or words), k is the min hash sketch size, and L is the number of sketches that are deployed.

a) Show that the following algorithm computes min hash values: let m be the number of images in the repository. Initialise all elements of a $kL \times m$ matrix h to ∞. The document-word matrix is scanned once in an arbitrary order: for each nonzero (j, i) element (meaning that word j appears in image i) and for each l with $1 \leq l \leq kL$ set $h[l, i]$ to $\pi_l(j)$ if $\pi_l(j) < h[l, i]$.

b) Assume π is an array of n integers that is initialised so that $\pi[l] = l$. Show that by assigning a random number to each array element and then sorting the array elements by the assigned random number you create a random permutation with uniform probability.

c) Initialise π as above. Show that by scanning π from $l = n$ down to $l = 1$ and, at each step, computing a random index i drawn uniformly and independently between 1 and l and then swapping the contents of $\pi[i]$ with $\pi[l]$ you create a random permutation with uniform probability.

CHAPTER 3

Content-based Retrieval in Depth

As features and distances are the main two ingredients for content-based retrieval, we will devote a whole section for each (3.2 and 3.3, respectively) and on tricks of the trade on how to standardise features and distances (3.4). Before delving into these, let us look at the global architecture (3.1) of how to use features and distances in principle. It will become apparent that the crux of the indexing problem is to compute nearest neighbours efficiently (3.5). With all this in hand, we can then look into the question of how to fuse evidence from the similarity with respect to different features that multimedia objects exhibit and how to merge search results from multiple query examples (3.6).

3.1 CONTENT-BASED RETRIEVAL ARCHITECTURE

The query-by-example paradigm extracts features from the query, which can be anything from a still image, a video clip, humming etc, and compares these with corresponding features in the database. The important bit is that both the query example and the database multimedia objects have undergone the same feature extraction mechanism. Figure 3.1 shows a typical architecture of such a system. The database indexing and similarity ranking tasks in Figure 3.1 identify the nearest neighbours in feature space with respect to a chosen distance function. It is sufficient to sort the distances of the query object to all database objects and only present as results the nearest neighbours, ie, the ones with the smallest distances to the objects in feature space.

The complexity of computing all distances and sorting them is $O(N \log(N))$ in time with N being the number of database objects. This can be brought down to $O(N)$ if one is only interested in the nearest, say, 100 neighbors. As such, this process is scalable in the sense that an increase of the database size requires a corresponding increase in the resources[1]. This naïve approach is very resource intense, though, as a single query requires a system to touch all feature vectors. This is neither practical, nor desirable for large databases. Section 3.5 looks at the indexing problem to compute nearest neighbours efficiently.

Both Figure 2.7 and the architecture sketch in Figure 3.1 suggest that there is only one monolithic feature space. However, it makes more sense to compute different features independently and in a modular fashion. Rather than one feature vector for a multimedia object m, one would have a number r of low-level features $f_1(m), f_2(m), \ldots, f_r(m)$, each of which would typically be a vector or numbers representing aspects like colour distribution, texture usage, shape encodings, musical timbre, pitch envelopes etc. Of course, one can always concatenate these individual feature vectors

---

[1]the technical definition of scalable is that the problem is $O(N)$ or better in time and memory

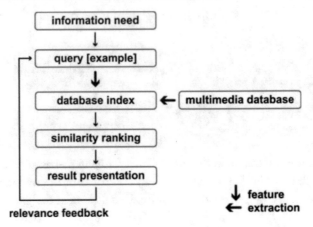

Figure 3.1: Content-based multimedia retrieval: generic architecture

to obtain a large monolithic one, but this is inelegant as different applications might want to focus on different features of the multimedia objects, and different individual feature vectors might call for different distance functions. Section 3.6 will look at ways to "fuse" query results from multiple feature spaces and at how to fuse comparisons over multiple query examples.

The architecture presented here is a typical, albeit basic, one; there are many variations and some radically different approaches that have been published in the past. A whole research field has gathered around the area of video and image retrieval as exemplified by the ACM Multimedia conference (ACM MM), the Conference on Image and Video Retrieval (CIVR), and Multimedia Information Retrieval (MIR), which used to be a workshop at ACM MM, has later developed into an ACM conference and is going to be merged with CIVR to form the ACM International Conference on Multimedia Retrieval (ICMR) from 2011. The TREC video evaluation workshop TRECVid has supported video retrieval research through independent, metric-based evaluation (see Subsection 5.4.4), while ImageCLEF has had this role for image retrieval research (see 5.4.5). There is another research field around music retrieval, as evidenced by the annual International Society for Music Information Retrieval Conference (ISMIR[2]), which has grown out from a symposium to a notable conference in 2003.

3.2   FEATURES

One common way of indexing multimedia is by creating summary statistics, which represent colour usage, texture composition, shape and structure, localisation, motion and audio properties. In this section, I discuss some of the widely used features and methods in more depth. Deselaers et al (2008) compare a large number of different image features for content-based image retrieval and give an overview of a large variety of image features. Features are not only relevant for retrieval

---

[2]http://www.ismir.net

tasks: Little and Rüger (2009) demonstrate how important the choice of the right features is for the automated image annotation task.

3.2.1   COLOUR HISTOGRAMS

Colour is a phenomenon of human perception. From a purely physical point of view, light emitted from surfaces follows a distribution of frequencies as seen in Figure 3.2. Each pure spectral frequency corresponds to a hue, all of which create the rainbow spectrum. The human eye has three different colour receptors that react to three different overlapping ranges of frequencies; their sensitivity peaks fall into the red, green and blue areas of the rainbow spectrum. Hence, human perception of colour is three-dimensional, and modelling colour as a mixture of red, green and blue is common. Virtually all colour spaces are three-dimensional (except for ones that utilise a fourth component for black), and so are colour histograms.

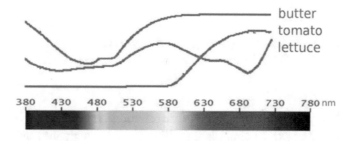

Figure 3.2: Spectral power of light emitted by different substances (imagined — not measured)

An example of a 3-dimensional colour histogram is depicted in Figure 3.3, which shows a crude summary of the colour usage in the original image. Here each of the red, green and blue colour axes in the so-called RGB space is subdivided into intervals yielding $4 \times 4 \times 4 = 64$ 3d colour bins; the proportion of pixels that are in each bin is represented by the size of a circle, which is positioned at the centre of a bin and coloured in correspondingly.

In general, the algorithm for computing histograms involves four steps as follows: (a) the underlying space is partitioned into cells — these can be 3d cells as in Figure 3.3 or 1d intensity intervals as in Figure 2.6; (b) each cell is associated with a unique integer, known as the histogram bin number or as the index of the histogram; (c) the number of occurrences in each cell is recorded using an integer counter each, eg, by sweeping over all pixels in the image, computing into which cell the pixel falls, and incrementing the corresponding bin counter; (d) the histogram is then normalised and, optionally, quantised: normalisation just requires to divide each bin counter h_i by the number n of image pixels ($n = wh$, where w is the width and h the height of the image). Quantisation is often required for space efficiency and typically done by assigning a k-bit integer to each histogram bin i through

$$i \mapsto \left\lfloor 2^k \frac{h_i}{n+1} \right\rfloor.$$

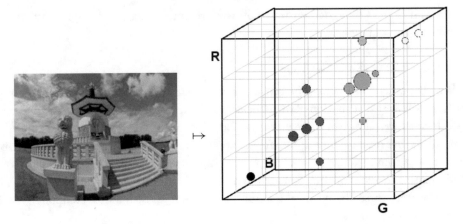

Figure 3.3: 3d colour histogram

We divide by $n + 1$ as opposed to n ensuring that $h_i/(n + 1)$ can never reach 1 (in which case i were to be mapped to 2^k, which is just outside the range of a k-bit integer).

3.2.2   STATISTICAL MOMENTS

Statistical moments are other ways to summarise distributions. If you wanted to express a quality of an object, say the intensities $p(i, j)$ of pixels at position (i, j), through one number alone you would most likely chose its average

$$\mu = \frac{1}{wh} \sum_{i=1}^{w} \sum_{j=1}^{h} p(i, j),$$

where w is the width and h the height of the image. The values

$$\overline{p}_k = \frac{1}{wh} \sum_{i=1}^{w} \sum_{j=1}^{h} (p(i, j) - \mu)^k \tag{3.1}$$

with $k > 1$ are known as the *central moments* of the quantity p, Indeed, the knowledge of all central moments and of μ is sufficient to reconstruct the distribution of p. $\overline{p}_2$ is also known as *variance*, while $\overline{p}_3$ and $\overline{p}_4$, respectively, are used to define (but not equal to) *skewness* and *kurtosis*. Skewness is a measure of the asymmetry of the probability distribution of the variable p: a negative value for a bell-shaped unimodal (ie, one peak) distribution indicates a long left tail where the mean is farther out in the left long tail than is the median; symmetric distribution bring about zero skewness, and the mean coincides with the median; finally, a positive value indicates a long right tail.[3] Kurtosis is a measure of how fat the tails of the distribution are: a high value means that much of the variance

---

[3]These rules of thumb can fail for multimodal distributions or those where the shorter tail is correspondingly "fatter" as to compensate the weight of the longer tail.

is owed to infrequent extreme deviations (a thin long tail), as opposed to frequent modestly-sized deviations.

In practical terms, the $\overline{p}_k$ have a highly different typical range owing to the "to the power of k" element in Equation 3.1. Hence, when using moments as parts of feature vectors, one normally deploys the k-th root in order to make the values comparable in size:

$$m_k = \text{sign}(\overline{p}_k)\sqrt[k]{|\overline{p}_k|} \tag{3.2}$$

The vector $(\mu, m_2, \ldots, m_l)$ of l floating point numbers roughly describes the underlying distribution and can be used as a feature vector. Note that $\overline{p}_k$ can be negative if k is odd, which explains why in Equation 3.2 the k-th root is applied to its absolute value. Nevertheless, m_k receives the same sign as $\overline{p}_k$ in Equation 3.2, and it is noteworthy that the feature vector $(\mu, m_2, \ldots, m_l)$ is neither normalised nor non-negative in contrast to histogram feature vectors.

3.2.3   TEXTURE HISTOGRAMS

Of course, the features of Figures 2.6 and 3.3 are very simple, and the features that we compute are normally more complex than that. For example, Howarth and Rüger (2005b) studied and devised ways to extract texture descriptions from images. Tamura et al (1978) have found out through psychological studies that we humans respond best to coarseness, contrast, and directionality as visualised in Figure 3.4, and to a lesser degree to line-likeness, regularity and roughness.

coarseness   contrast   directionality

Figure 3.4: Textures

Unlike colour, which is a property of a pixel, texture is a property of a region of pixels, so we need to look at an area around a pixel before we can assign a texture to that pixel. Figure 3.5 is an example, how we compute for each point in an image (by considering a window around this point) a coarseness (C) value, a contrast value (N) and a directionality value (D). These values can be assembled into a single false-colour image, where the red, blue and green channels of an ordinary image are replaced by C, N and D, respectively. This expresses visually the use and perception of texture in an image. From the false-colour texture image, we can then compute 3d texture histograms exactly in the same way as we do for colour images.

Textures are normally computed from greyscale images — although there is nothing to prevent one from extracting textures from colour channels or from studying the patterns that colours of similar greyscale introduce.

We will first study in depth how Tamura texture features can be computed.

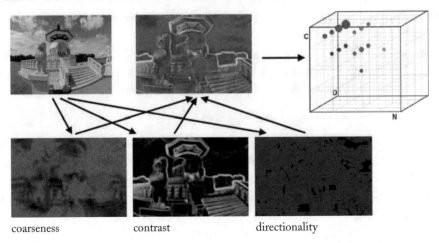

coarseness   contrast   directionality

Figure 3.5: 3d texture diagram via false-colour images

Tamura Texture Features

Coarseness has a direct relationship to scale and repetition rates and was seen by Tamura et al (1978) as the most fundamental texture feature. An image will contain textures at several scales; coarseness aims to identify the largest size of these scales, even where a smaller regular pattern exists. First, we take a moving average at every point over $2^k \times 2^k$ windows, $k < 6$. This average at the point (x, y) is

$$a_k(i, j) = \sum_{i'=i-2^{k-1}}^{i+2^{k-1}-1} \sum_{j'=j-2^{k-1}}^{j+2^{k-1}-1} \frac{p(i', j')}{2^{2k}},$$

where $p(i, j)$ is the grey level at the image pixel coordinates (i, j). Then one computes the bigger of the horizontal and vertical differences of a_k at the edge of the window:

$$c_k(i, j) = \max(\ |a_k(i - 2^{k-1}, j) - a_k(i + 2^{k-1}, j)|,$$

$$|a_k(i, j - 2^{k-1}) - a_k(i, j + 2^{k-1})|)$$

This value will differ with k, and the

$$\hat{k}(i, j) = \text{argmax}_k\ c_k(i, j)$$

that maximises c_k indicates the biggest detected scale $2^{\hat{k}(i,j)}$ at the point (i, j). The coarseness value for a whole picture is then averaged as

$$\text{coarseness} = \frac{1}{wh} \sum_{(i,j)} 2^{\hat{k}(i,j)}.$$

When carrying out these calculations one has to be careful not to exceed the area of the original image. The moving average a_k can only be computed in a smaller area, and c_k can only be computed in a smaller area still, see Figure 3.6.

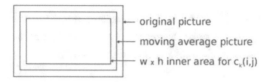

    — original picture

    — moving average picture

    — w x h inner area for $c_x(i,j)$

Figure 3.6: Domain over which coarseness can be computed

Contrast aims to capture the dynamic range of grey levels in an image together with the polarisation of the distribution of black and white. The first quantity is measured using the variance

$$\sigma^2 = \frac{1}{wh} \sum_{(i,j)} (p(i, j) - \bar{p}_1)^2$$

of grey levels, while the second quantity is obtained by the

$$\alpha_4 = \bar{p}_4/\sigma^4 = \frac{1}{wh} \sum_{(i,j)} (p(i, j) - \bar{p}_1)^4/\sigma^4.$$

$\bar{p}_1$ stands for the average grey value. The contrast measure is defined as

$$\text{contrast} = \sigma/(\alpha_4)^n$$

Experimentally, Tamura found $n = 1/4$ to give the closest agreement to human measurements.

Directionality is a global property over a region. The feature described does not aim to differentiate between different orientations or patterns, but it measures the total degree of directionality. At each pixel, a gradient

$$g = \begin{pmatrix} \Delta_h \\ \Delta_v \end{pmatrix} \text{ with}$$

$$\Delta_h = \sum_{k\in\{-1,0,1\}} p(i + 1, j + k) - p(i - 1, j + k) \text{ and}$$

$$\Delta_v = \sum_{k\in\{-1,0,1\}} p(i + k, j + 1) - p(i + k, j - 1)$$

is computed. The gradient computation corresponds to convolving the image with two simple masks for edge detection,

$$\begin{pmatrix} -1 & 0 & 1 \\ -1 & 0 & 1 \\ -1 & 0 & 1 \end{pmatrix} \text{ and } \begin{pmatrix} 1 & 1 & 1 \\ 0 & 0 & 0 \\ -1 & -1 & -1 \end{pmatrix},$$

respectively. The gradient g is then transformed into bi-polar coordinates

$$(|g|, \phi) = \left(\frac{|\Delta_h| + |\Delta_v|}{2}, \tan^{-1}\left(\frac{\Delta_v}{\Delta_h} \right) + \frac{\pi}{2} \right),$$

which reveal size and direction of the gradient. The next step is to compute a histogram over quantised angles for those gradients with a size $|g|$ larger than a certain threshold. The histogram bin $h\phi(k)$ counts the proportion of those pixels above threshold for which

$$\frac{2k - 1}{2n} < \phi/\pi \leq \frac{2k + 1}{2n}(\bmod\ 1).$$

n determines the granularity of the histogram of edge directions. This histogram reflects the degree of directionality, see Figure 3.7. To extract a measure, the sharpness of the histogram peaks is computed from their second moments.

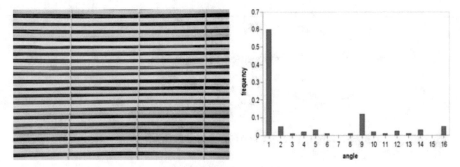

Figure 3.7: Example image and directionality histogram

3.2.4 SHAPE

Shape is commonly defined as an equivalence class of geometric objects invariant under translations, rotations and scale changes that keep the aspect ratio. Many retrieval applications require global scale invariance, ie, relative sizes are still meaningful. Hence, I will not require scale invariance in the following when looking at shapes. Strict scale invariance would imply that the sizes of objects do not matter at all.

Shape representations can preserve the underlying information, so the shape can be reconstructed or they can simply aim at keeping interesting aspects. The former type is used for compression while the latter may be sufficient for retrieval. There are a number of boundary-based features than can be extracted — these ignore the interior of shapes including holes in it. Other shape features are region-based.

This section assumes that we have a representation of the shape to be analysed at hand. It is normally non-trivial to separate background objects from foreground objects in pixel-images, and this theme is outside the scope of this book. There are some cases, however, where this separation is easily possible because the shape objects already exist in parameterised form, for example, as vector graphics, or in different layers owing to the production method of the multimedia object. Some media, for instance, comic strips or cartoon movies, lend themselves to simple object separation.

Boundary-based Shape Features

The *boundary* of a 2d shape can be described mathematically in terms of a parameterised curve:

$$B: [0, 1] \rightarrow \mathbb{R}^2$$
$$t \mapsto (x(t), y(t))$$

Normally, one would expect B to be continuous, and a continuous boundary B is called closed if and only if $B(0) = B(1)$.

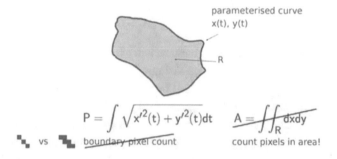

Figure 3.8: Perimeter and area of a shape

The *perimeter of a shape* is the length

$$P = \int \sqrt{x'(t)^2 + y'(t)^2} dt$$

of its boundary $t \mapsto (x(t), y(t))$. Here f' denotes the derivative $\partial f / \partial t$ of a function f with respect to t. If you have a representation of a boundary in form of pixels, it is normally not good enough to count the pixels in this representation, as the digitisation of the mathematical line consumes a different amount of pixels at different angles and apparent line thicknesses, see Figure 3.8. This is in stark contrast to the best way of determining the *area of a shape* that can easily be approximated by counting the pixels that it fills.

The *convexity of a shape* is one important characteristics. A convex region is one, where the connecting line between any two points of the region lies within it. It is always possible to construct a convex hull from a region, see Figure 3.9. The ratio of the perimeter of the convex hull and the perimeter of the original boundary is called *convexity*. It is 1 for convex shapes and less than 1 for non-convex shapes.

A similar idea is behind the characteristics of the circularity of a shape, which is defined as

$$T = 4\pi \frac{A}{P^2},$$

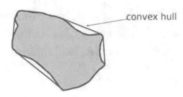

Figure 3.9: Convexity and convex hull

where A is the area of the shape and P is its perimeter. The circularity of a shape is 1 for a circle and less than one for other shapes.

Corners in a parameterised curve are places with a high curvature

$$c = \frac{x'y'' - y'x''}{(x'^2 + y'^2)^{3/2}}.$$

The number of corners is another possible characteristics for a shape.

An early boundary representation with strings that can be used for recognition purposes is that of *chain codes* proposed by Freeman (1961). They approximate curves with a sequence of vectors lying on a square grid. In its simplest form, each pixel in a curve has eight neighbours, numbered counter-clockwise from 0 to 7 starting with the neighbour to the right, see Figure 3.10. A line can be encoded by following the pixels in the line one by one, each time making a note of the neighbour number. Figure 3.10 illustrates this with the small circle-like contour. We begin encoding it at a pixel in the middle-left, move up one position (2), move diagonally up to the right (1), then to right (0), and so on. For closed curves the resulting chain code depends on where we started and in which direction. One way out of this is to assign the representation with the smallest number, here 007765434321.

$$\begin{array}{ccc} 3 & 2 & 1 \\ 4 & \bullet & 0 \\ 5 & 6 & 7 \end{array} \qquad = 210077654343$$

Figure 3.10: Freeman chain code

However, this representation is still not rotation invariant. To achieve the latter one can transform a chain code $(f_1, f_2, \ldots, f_n)$ into a *difference chain code* via a sequence of angles

$$a_i = (f_{i+1} - f_i) \mod 8 \qquad (3.3)$$

rather than directions. Figure 3.11 illustrates the 8 different angles with their codes from 0 to 7 and that the difference chain code of the rotated figure remains the same.

Finally, as seen in Figure 3.12, one can then summarise individual curves into histograms.

A well-established technique to describe closed planar curves is the use of Fourier descriptors (Zahn and Roskies, 1972; Persoon and Fu, 1977). Using the Fourier descriptors one can achieve

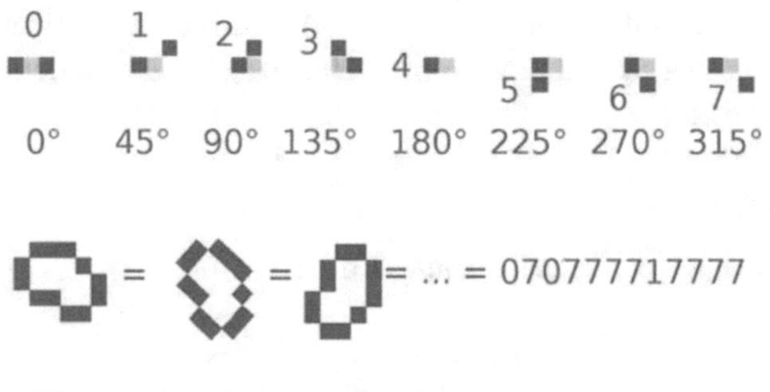

0   1   2   3   4
                                    5   6   7

0°   45°   90°   135°   180°   225°   270°   315°

= = = ... = 070777717777

Figure 3.11: Difference chain codes are rotation invariant

070777717777

Figure 3.12: Histogram of difference chain code

representational invariance with respect to a variety of affine transformations; Wallace and Wintz (1980) have successfully used these descriptors for recognition tasks.

For the computation of Fourier descriptors, the contour pixels at coordinates (x, y) need to be represented as complex numbers $z = x + jy$. For closed contours, we get a periodic function which can be expanded into a convergent Fourier series. Specifically, let Fourier descriptor C_k be defined as the kth discrete Fourier transform coefficient

$$C_k = \sum_{n=0}^{N-1} (z_n e^{\frac{-2\pi jkn}{N}}),$$

$-N/2 \leq k < N/2$, which we compute from the sequence of complex numbers $z_0, z_1, \ldots, z_{N-1}$ where N is the number of contour points. To characterise contour properties any constant number of these Fourier descriptors can be used. The most interesting descriptors are those of the lower frequencies as these tend to capture the general shape of the object. Translation invariance is achieved by discarding C_0, rotation and starting point invariance by further using only absolute values of the descriptors, and scaling invariance is brought about by dividing the other descriptors by, say, $|C_1|$. The final feature vector has the form

$$\left(\frac{|C_{-L}|}{|C_1|}, \ldots, \frac{|C_{-1}|}{|C_1|}, \frac{|C_2|}{|C_1|}, \ldots, \frac{|C_L|}{|C_1|} \right)^T,$$

where L is an arbitrary constant between 2 and $N/2 - 1$. The thus derived feature vector has a good theoretical foundation and a clear interpretation, which makes it easy to decide on granularity and size of the vector to chose.

Region-based Shape Descriptors

We model a bounded region of a shape as a function

$$f : \mathbb{R}^2 \;\; \rightarrow \;\; \{0, 1\}$$
$$(x, y) \;\; \mapsto \;\; \begin{cases} 1 & \text{if pixel at } (x, y) \text{ is on} \\ 0 & \text{otherwise.} \end{cases}$$

It turns out that the knowledge of all its 2d moments

$$M_{ij} = \sum_{(x,y)} x^i y^j f(x, y), \quad i, j \in \mathbb{N},$$

is sufficient to reconstruct f and with it the region. Two useful entities are M_{00}, which is the area of the region, and

$$(\bar{x}, \bar{y}) = \left(\frac{M_{10}}{M_{00}}, \frac{M_{01}}{M_{00}} \right),$$

which is the centre of mass of the region, see Figure 3.13.

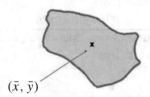

$$(\bar{x}, \bar{y})$$

Figure 3.13: Centre of mass expressed with 2d moments

The *central moments*

$$C_{ij} = \sum_{(x,y)} (x - \bar{x})^i (y - \bar{y})^j f(x, y),$$

which are centred around $(\bar{x}, \bar{y})$, are translation invariant by construction. If these moments are then divided by the right power of the region's area then the ensuing *normalised central moments*

$$c_{ij} = C_{ij} / M_{00}^{1+(i+j)/2}$$

are both translation and scaling invariant. It is possible to construct the following 7 descriptors, which are rotation invariant in addition:

$$
\begin{aligned}
I_1 &= c_{02} + c_{20} \\
I_2 &= (c_{20} - c_{02})^2 + 4c_{11}^2 \\
I_3 &= (c_{30} - 3c_{12})^2 + (3c_{21} - c_{03})^2 \\
I_4 &= (c_{30} + c_{12})^2 + (c_{21} + c_{03})^2 \\
I_5 &= (c_{30} - 3c_{12})(c_{30} + c_{12})((c_{30} + c_{12})^2 - 3(c_{21} + c_{03})^2) + \\
&\quad (3c_{21} - c_{03})(c_{21} + c_{03})(3(c_{30} + c_{12})^2 - (c_{21} + c_{03})^2) \\
I_6 &= (c_{20} - c_{02})((c_{30} + c_{12})^2 - (c_{21} + c_{03})^2) + \\
&\quad 4c_{11}(c_{30} + c_{12})(c_{21} + c_{03}) \\
I_7 &= (3c_{21} - c_{03})(c_{30} + c_{12})((c_{30} + c_{12})^2 - 3(c_{21} + c_{03})^2) + \\
&\quad (3c_{12} - c_{30})(c_{21} + c_{03})(3(c_{30} + c_{12})^2 - (c_{21} + c_{03})^2)
\end{aligned}
$$

These 7 numbers are called *invariant moments*. I_2 is also known as eccentricity. Although they are useful descriptors for shapes, invariant moments are not very expressive, and it is not clear how one could use these to scale up complex shapes. One can compute other useful properties of shapes with normalised central moments, though: the *orientation of a shape*, an angle indicating its main axis, is given by

$$
\phi = \frac{1}{2} \tan^{-1}\left(\frac{2c_{11}}{c_{20} - c_{02}}\right),
$$

see Figure 3.14.

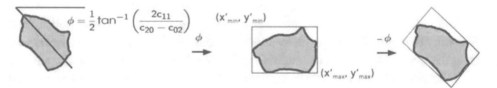

Figure 3.14: Bounding box computation via orientation angle ϕ

Rotating the shape by this angle ϕ

$$
\begin{pmatrix} x' \\ y' \end{pmatrix} = \begin{pmatrix} \cos(\phi) & \sin(\phi) \\ -\sin(\phi) & \cos(\phi) \end{pmatrix} \begin{pmatrix} x \\ y \end{pmatrix}
$$

makes it easy to determine a minimal bounding box. Let $(x'_{\min}, y'_{\min})$ and $(x'_{\max}, y'_{\max})$ be the extreme coordinates of the rotated bounding box, then you can identify the coordinates of the minimal bounding box by rotating about $-\phi$.

All of the above-mentioned shape representations have in common that they can be stored as a simple vector. More elaborate shape representations have been introduced some of which are the curvature scale space representation or the spline curve approximation which require sophisticated shape matching techniques (del Bimbo and Pala, 1997).

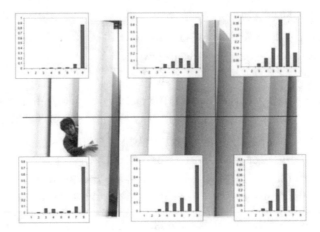

Figure 3.15: The feature vector of tiled images

3.2.5   SPATIAL INFORMATION

Tiled Histograms

Histograms as in Figure 2.6 are useful instruments, but they are very crude indicators of similarity. For example an eight-bin histogram of intensity values of an image is a simple approximation of its brightness distribution, and many images do indeed share the same histogram. Figure 3.16 shows a woman in the middle of bright column sculptures, but an image of a skier in snow is likely to have the same intensity histogram. The other disadvantage of global histograms computed over the whole image is that they lose all locality information. One simple solution is to tile an image into $n \times m$ rectangles of the same size, each of which creates a histogram (see Figure 3.15). The full feature vector is then the concatenation of the feature vectors of individual tiles and, in this case, contains $6 \cdot 8$ numbers.

Designing Different Areas of Importance

Different areas in images carry different importance: computing separate histograms for its centre and the border region allows one to focus more on one than on the other. Figure 3.16 is an example of a centre-border intensity histogram, where two histograms are computed: as the centre area is much bigger than the border area the corresponding proportion of pixels that fall into centre area intensity ranges is typically larger than for intensity ranges of the border area. This gives the centre extra weight.

The photographic composition principle of the "rule of thirds" implies that lines or objects of interest work best in a photograph if they are off-centre, roughly one third or two thirds into the

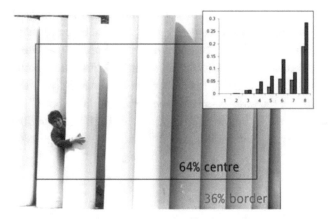

Figure 3.16: Centre-border intensity histogram of an image

image. A similar, but slightly more evolved aesthetic principle, suggests composing interesting objects at points that divide the height or width of an image at the golden ratio of $(\sqrt{5} - 1)/2 \approx 0.618$ as opposed to 2/3. It is a surprising fact that the 25% of the central area of an image still captures all these points of interest with a generous margin. Figure 3.17 contrasts global histograms with three other schemes that aim at recovering crude localisation information. *Focal* histograms only consider the 25% interior of any image, while *central* histograms put much weight on the main histogram of the central 50% area but retain some information about the background in four sub-histograms of less weight. Finally, *local* histograms create five sub-histograms of equal weight, four of which are around the possible four quadrants of interest, while the fifth caters for the background.

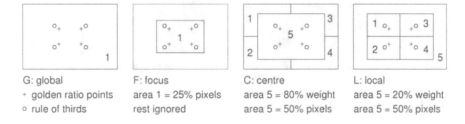

Figure 3.17: Different strategies to capture essential areas in photographs

Structure Histograms

The MPEG-7 *colour structure histogram* folds the frequency of a colour with information how concentrated or scattered it occurs in an image. In the same way as in global colour histograms, each pixel is assigned a corresponding bin (either as 1d intensity or 3d colour bin). However, here a gliding 8×8 window moves over the image, and each histogram bin counts the *number of overlapping windows* that contain at least one pixel of the corresponding bin. An image that has a concentrated occurrence of blue in the top will have a smaller count for the blue cell than another image, where the same number of blue pixels are peppered across the whole image. Messing et al (2001) claim that, for this reason, the colour structure descriptor outperforms other colour descriptors. It should be noted that the structuring element of the colour structure descriptor is applicable to all qualities of spatial arrangements, eg, the false-colour texture representation above.

Normalisation is through dividing by the number of different window positions; each component is thus between 0 and 1, but the sum can, in rare cases, be as large as 64, the number of pixels in the gliding window.

Localised Features

One quite successful idea to exploit local structure is to compute points of interest. These are salient points in images that give rise to encoding features in limited area. Figure 3.18 illustrates the idea, but algorithms that compute points of interests normally compute many more regions.

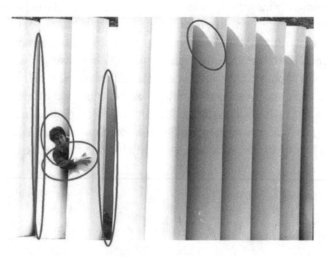

Figure 3.18: Points and regions of interest

Lowe (1999, 2004) has developed a popular *scale-invariant feature transform* (SIFT) that detects and encodes local features in images. The first step is to detect candidate points of interest in an image by convolving a 2d Gaussian function of different scale σ with the image (basically a smoothing or blurring of the image with different radius) and taking differences of the resulting function (blurred image) at each point with respect to slightly different scales σ and $k\sigma$. The extrema of this function, called difference of Gaussians, indicate candidate points of interest. From these keypoints are localised and orientations assigned, which serve as a local reference coordinate system. The final features that are extracted from this area are computed relative to this local reference, so that they are encoded in a scale, rotation and location invariant manner. A typical image exhibits in the order of 2000 key-points.

Using points of interests with localised features allows one to quantise the latter into so called *visual words*. Being quantised one can deploy the same type of retrieval techniques that are so successful for text retrieval: inverted-file indices. Localised features and quantisation is a very powerful combination for duplicate detection.

3.2.6   OTHER FEATURE TYPES

There is a sheer abundance of different feature types. Above were a mere selection of features for colour, texture and shape features that are useful for visual still image retrieval. They demonstrate the type of processing from counting to Fourier transforms that is typical for low-level processing.

It should be noted that MPEG-7 (see Section 2.1 on page 16) has defined the following set of features for low-level audiovisual content description:

- colour: colour space, colour quantization, dominant colour(s), scalable colour, colour layout, colour-structure descriptor, GoF/GoP colour
- texture: homogeneous texture, texture browsing, edge histogram
- shape: region shape, contour shape, shape 3d
- motion: camera motion, motion trajectory, parametric motion, motion activity

I have described a single one of them, the colour-structure descriptor, just above.

A deep treatment of music and audio features is beyond the scope of this book. I refer to Liu et al (1998), who reviewed a good range of audio features.

3.3   DISTANCES

Most of above features create real-valued vectors of a fixed dimension n, where distance computation is straightforward. We will first introduce standard distance measures that work component-wise such as the Minkowski distance, then distances that include cross-component correlations such as the Mahalanobis distance between vectors, followed by statistical and probabilistic distance measures including the popular mover's distance between probability distributions, and those that work on a string level.

3.3.1   GEOMETRIC COMPONENT-WISE DISTANCES

Let $v, w \in \mathbb{R}^n$. The so-called *Minkowski norm*

$$
\begin{aligned}
L_p : \mathbb{R}^n &\rightarrow [0, \infty) \\
w &\mapsto |w|_p = \left(\sum_{i=1}^{n} |w_i|^p \right)^{1/p}
\end{aligned}
$$

induces a distance

$$d_p(v, w) = \mathrm{L}_p(w - v).$$

L_p is a norm for all real values $p \in [1, \infty]$ meaning $\mathrm{L}_p(v) = 0$ if and only if $v = 0$; $\mathrm{L}_p(av) = |a|\,\mathrm{L}_p(v)$ for all $a \in \mathbb{R}$ and $v \in \mathbb{R}^n$, and $\mathrm{L}_p(v + w) \leq \mathrm{L}_p(v) + \mathrm{L}_p(w)$ for all $v, w \in \mathbb{R}^n$. The latter is also known as triangle inequality. The induced distance fulfills corresponding axioms.

One special case for $p = 2$ is also known as the *Euclidean norm*, which is the length of a line between points in space. Another special case, $p = 1$, yields the *Manhattan norm*, which corresponds to the total length of a sequence of lines parallel to the coordinate axes from point v to point w. $d_1(v, w)$ is called Manhattan distance, because cars in Manhattan can only go along the grid system of perpendicular streets and avenues (ignoring the existence of the diagonal Broadway). As p increases beyond 2, the sum in $d_p(v, w)$ is more and more dominated by the largest difference $|v_i - w_i|$ of components, and as p approaches infinity $d_p(v, w)$ will be identical to the maximum of all values $|v_i - w_i|$ over i. Hence L_∞ is also called *maximum norm* or *Chebyshev norm*. However, this norm is not particularly useful for multimedia retrieval as it implies that the distance between two media representations v and w is solely determined by the biggest non-matching component, which may as well be an outlier, and hence irrelevant to our perception of similarity. It turns out that a p at the lower end of the spectrum normally give better retrieval results owing to a larger emphasis on components that actually match.

This has led to exploring values of p in the area of $(0, 1)$ for nearest neighbour search (Aggarwal et al, 2001). Technically, L_p is no longer a norm for $p < 1$ as the triangle inequality is violated, but it is still possible to order the induced dissimilarity[4] values accordingly. Howarth and Rüger (2005a) have found best retrieval results for many feature vectors types with p values between 0.5 and 0.75.

A special dissimilarity measure for histograms, called partial histogram intersection, is given by

$$d_{\mathrm{phi}}(v, w) = 1 - \frac{\sum_i \min(v_i, w_i)}{\max\left(\mathrm{L}_1(v), \mathrm{L}_1(w)\right)}.$$

In this context, v and w are not necessarily normalised histograms, but they ought to be in the same range to make sense. The components of v and w are expected to be non-negative. This dissimilarity measure is very popular for normalised histogram features, and for those equivalent to the Manhattan distance (see Exercise 3.7.6).

There are other geometrically motivated distances between vectors, for example, the *Canberra distance*

$$d_{\mathrm{Can}}(v, w) = \sum_{i=1}^{n} \frac{|v_i - w_i|}{|v_i| + |w_i|},$$

which is very sensitive for components near zero. Note that the term $|v_i - w_i|/(|v_i| + |w_i|)$ needs to be replaced by zero if both v_i and w_i are zero.

---

[4]we prefer the term dissimilarity when not all mathematical axioms for distances are valid

A common dissimilarity measure in Information Retrieval is the *cosine dissimilarity* defined as

$$d_{\cos}(v, w) = 1 - \frac{v \cdot w}{L_2(v)\, L_2(w)}$$

named after the fact that the normalised scalar product $v \cdot w / L_2(v)\, L_2(w)$ between v and w is the cosine of the angle between the vectors v and w. $d_{\cos}$ is not a distance, as one cannot conclude from $d_{\cos}(v, w) = 0$ that $v = w$. This is owing to the fact that the length of v and w is irrelevant and only their direction is used for the computation.

The *Bray-Curtis dissimilarity* is derived from the Manhattan distance as

$$d_{\mathrm{BC}}(v, w) = \frac{d_1(v, w)}{d_1(v, -w)} = \frac{\sum_i |v_i - w_i|}{\sum_i |v_i + w_i|}$$

and approaches infinity as v approaches $-w$.

A less usual measure is given by the *squared chord dissimilarity*,

$$d_{\mathrm{sc}}(v, w) = \sum_{i=1}^{n} (\sqrt{v_i} - \sqrt{w_i})^2,$$

which seems to have been used in paleontological studies and in pollen data analysis, both with little theoretical justification. In comparative evaluation, the squared chord measure does remarkably well though (Hu et al, 2008). Please note that the squared chord dissimilarity cannot work with negative components; it should be replaced with a modified version

$$d_{\mathrm{msc}}(v, w) = \sum_{i=1}^{n} \left(\mathrm{sign}(v_i)\sqrt{|v_i|} - \mathrm{sign}(w_i)\sqrt{|w_i|} \right)^2$$

instead.

3.3.2   GEOMETRIC QUADRATIC DISTANCES

If two images only differ by lighting, then their respective colour histograms will be shifted. All pixels that would end up in the white bin in one image might end up in the light-yellow bin in the other image. Component-wise distance measures will not recognise that the light-yellow bin is not so different from the white bin: they only see a mismatch, and the white pixels might as well have ended up in the dark-blue bin.

One way to recognise the closeness of the feature components that the individual bins represent is through a quadratic matrix A that maps two bins to a number that represents how similar their underlying features are. In the case of colour histograms, A_{ij} might be set to a similarity of the colour triplets that represent the bins in, say, RGB colour space $[0, 1]^3 \ni (r, g, b)$:

$$A_{ij} = 1 - |(r_i, g_i, b_i) - (r_j, g_j, b_j)|_\infty = 1 - \max(|r_i - r_j|, |g_i - g_j|, |b_i - b_j|)$$

is one such example of how the matrix A could be created. The *feature quadratic distance* is then defined as

$$d_{fq}(v, w) = \sqrt{(v - w)^t A(v - w)}.$$

This distance measure is identical in form to the *Mahalanobis distance* between two random vectors v and w of the same distribution with the covariance matrix S, only that A is replaced by S^{-1}. If S (or A) is the unit matrix then d_{fq} collapses to the Euclidean distance d_2. If the co-variance matrix S is diagonal (or A is), then d_{fq} is the so-called normalised Euclidean distance

$$d_2^{\sigma}(v, w) = \sqrt{\sum_i \frac{(v_i - w_i)^2}{\sigma_i^2}}.$$

Since the histogram quadratic distance computes the cross similarity between features, it is computationally more expensive than component-wise distance measures.

3.3.3   STATISTICAL DISTANCES

Histograms approximate distributions of the underlying quantity, and normalised histograms can be interpreted as probability distributions themselves. There is a number of dissimilarity measures that are derived from a statistical motivation. For example, the χ^2 statistics

$$d_{\chi^2}(v, w) = \sum_i \frac{(v_i - m_i)^2}{m_i}$$

with $m = (v + w)/2$ measures how different two frequency distributions are.

A whole raft of distances can be defined by converting normalised histograms v into cumulative histograms $\hat{v}$ via

$$\hat{v}_i = \sum_{j \leq i} v_j.$$

Plugging cumulative histograms into L_p defines cumulative distances

$$\hat{d}_p(v, w) = d_p(\hat{v}, \hat{w}) = L_p(\hat{v} - \hat{w}).$$

$\hat{d}_1$ is also known as *match distance*, $\hat{d}_2$ is known as *Cramér-von-Mises-type distance*, while $\hat{d}_\infty$ is also known as *Kolmogorov-Smirnov distance* (Puzicha et al, 1997). Note, however, that cumulative histograms — and hence cumulative distances — are only defined for histograms over a one-dimensional space, i.e., histograms with bins that can be linearly ordered. 3d colour histograms, for example, do not have a cumulative version, as it is not immediately clear how the two colours j and i could be intrinsically ordered such that $j \leq i$.

Another measure, derived from the Pearson correlation coefficient, is defined as

$$d_{pcc}(v, w) = 1 - |r|,$$

where the correlation coefficient

$$r = \frac{n \sum_{i=1}^{n} v_i w_i - \left(\sum_{i=1}^{n} v_i\right) \left(\sum_{i=1}^{n} w_i\right)}{\sqrt{\left[n \sum_{i=1}^{n} v_i^2 - \left(\sum_{i=1}^{n} v_i\right)^2\right]\left[n \sum_{i=1}^{n} w_i^2 - \left(\sum_{i=1}^{n} w_i\right)^2\right]}}.$$

is a number between -1 and 1, where -1 corresponds to a strong negative correlation (small v_i correspond to large w_i and vice versa), $r = 0$ corresponds to uncorrelated distributions r and w, while positive values for r indicate a positive correlation. Note that both strong positive and strong negative correlation of v and w yield small distances.

3.3.4   PROBABILISTIC DISTANCE MEASURES

The *Kullback-Leibler divergence* expresses the degree of discrepancy between two probability distributions v and w, and measures the extra information needed to express a sample from the "true" distribution v when one encodes them with samples from an approximation distribution w. For discrete random vectors v and w, their Kullback-Leibler divergence is defined as

$$d_{\text{KL}}(v, w) = \sum_i v_i \log \frac{v_i}{w_i}.$$

d_{KL} is not a distance: it is not even symmetric and grows arbitrarily big for any component of w approaching 0, which makes the Kullback-Leibler divergence unsuitable for many feature types that tend to have vanishing components. This measure can be made symmetric through the definition of the *Jensen-Shannon divergence*

$$d_{\text{JS}}(v, w) = (d_{\text{KL}}(v, m) + d_{\text{KL}}(w, m))/2,$$

where $m = (v + w)/2$. The Jensen-Shannon divergence has the added benefit of being finite. It needs to be re-emphasised that both the Kullback-Leibler and the Jensen-Shannon divergence are only defined for probability vectors, ie, with non-negative components that sum to one. These measures would not be suitable for a number of feature types, for example, those that describe distributions with their central moments, as they can be negative.

Another intuitive distance measure between two probability distributions over a space D is the *earth mover's distance*: here, one distribution v is defined as an amount of earth piled up in regions of D, while the other distribution w is defined as an amount of holes distributed in regions of D. The earth mover's distance between v and w is defined as the minimum cost of moving the piles of earth into the holes, cost being defined as the amount of earth moved times the distance it is moved.

It is important to realise that the distributions are defined over some space D with a distance called *ground distance*. For instance, v and w might be colour distributions over a colour space, say, RGB, where the ground distance is defined as some distance between colours. In this sense, the earth mover's distance is similarly expressive as the feature quadratic distance, but it has the advantage of not needing a fixed partition of the space D that histograms would give. Instead a distribution

v can be defined as a list of n^v cluster centres $c_i^v \in D$ and corresponding masses $m_i^v \in [0, 1]$ (eg, proportion of pixels that fall into this cluster):

$$v = ((c_1^v, m_1^v), (c_2^v, m_2^v), \ldots, (c_{n^v}^v, m_{n^v}^v))$$

These lists are also known as *signatures*; note that they have variable length and generalise the notion of histograms. Figure 3.19 illustrates two signatures v, w over $D = \mathbb{R}^2$ and shows the optimal way of morphing v into w.

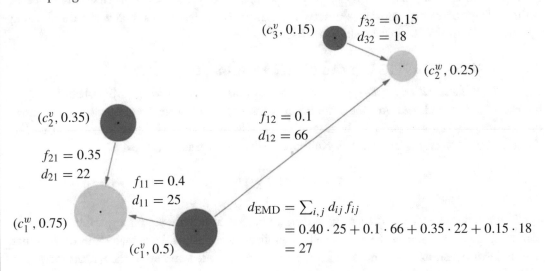

Figure 3.19: Earth mover's distance between two signatures

Although the earth mover's distance can be defined where both signatures have a different total mass, we restrict ourselves to signatures with a total mass of 1 each. A formal way of describing the earth mover's distance between any two such signatures v and w involves the definition of a ground distance

$$d_{ij} = d(c_i^v, c_j^w)$$

and a flow f_{ij} of mass between the i-th cluster centre of v and the j-th cluster centre of w. This flow is subject to the constraints

$$f_{ij} \geq 0 \tag{3.4}$$

$$\sum_j f_{ij} = m_i^v \tag{3.5}$$

$$\sum_i f_{ij} = m_j^w \tag{3.6}$$

for all $1 \leq i \leq n^v$ and all $1 \leq j \leq n^w$. (3.4) stipulates that mass can only flow in the direction from v to w, ie, from the piles of earth into the holes, (3.5) that the total flow from a pile must be equal its size, while (3.6) means that the total flow into a hole must be equal to the capacity of the hole.

The earth mover's distance is now defined as the minimum cost to shift all mass from v to w with respect to all possible flows f that fulfill constraints (3.4)–(3.6):

$$d_{\mathrm{EMD}}(v, w) = \min_f \sum_{i,j} f_{ij} d_{ij}$$

Figure 3.19 illustrates one such cost computation. The problem of finding the flow f with the minimal cost is also known as transportation problem for which efficient algorithms exist. Yossi Rubner distributes a C programme[5] based on an algorithm from Hillier and Lieberman's textbook (1990).

Rubner et al (2000) showed that d_{EMD} applied to mass 1 signatures is a distance, ie, fulfills the triangle inequality if the ground distance is a distance; they also examined the use of the earth mover's distance for image retrieval where it outperforms other distances. While the earth mover's distance is made for signatures it can, in theory, be applied to histograms as well. However, large histogram bins bring about quantisation errors while small bins make the transportation algorithm run slowly. It appears to be advantageous to apply the earth mover's distance to signatures rather than fixed-bin histograms.

3.3.5   ORDINAL AND NOMINAL DISTANCES

When feature values are non-numeric, ie, general strings, none of the above distance measures can be used. An exception to this are ordinal labels, ie, those which can be ranked or have a numeric rating scale attached. These labels can be mapped to numbers: for example, *small*, *normal*, *large* and *extra large* can be mapped to their ranks 4, 3, 2, and 1, respectively.

In all other cases, the string attributes are a known as nominal labels and a matching coefficient

$$m(v, w) = \sum_i \delta(v_i, w_i) \ \text{ with } \ \delta(v_i, w_i) = \begin{cases} 1 & \text{if } v_i = w_i \\ 0 & \text{otherwise} \end{cases}$$

can be transformed into a distance measure

$$d_{\mathrm{mc}}(v, w) = 1 - \frac{m(v, w)}{n}.$$

The matching coefficient simply $m(v, w)$ counts the number of coordinates, whose strings match.

The same matching coefficient can be used with binary feature components. There is an important case, though, where the binary data are *asymmetric*, ie, the outcome one expresses a rare and important case while zero encodes a normal and frequent situation. This is the case in sparse vector representations of "bags of words", where a text document is represented as a vector telling which words out of the whole repository vocabulary are present and which are not. In this representation, d_{mc} between two documents would decrease for each word that both do *not* contain.

[5]http://robotics.stanford.edu/~rubner/emd/default.htm

For example, the fact that two documents *did not* contain the word "antidisestablishmentarianism" would make them less distant in the same way as if the word "electroencephalogram" *did* occur in both. This is clearly not desirable! It is best to ignore matching frequent cases in those asymmetric encodings as is done in the Jaccard distance

$$d_{\text{Jaccard}}(v, w) = 1 - \frac{m^1(v, w)}{n - m^0(v, w)},$$

where $m^b(v, w)$ counts the number of coordinates, whose binary value is both b:

$$m^b(v, w) = \sum_i \delta(v_i, b)\delta(w_i, b) \text{ with } \delta(a, b) = \begin{cases} 1 & \text{if } a = b \\ 0 & \text{otherwise} \end{cases}$$

3.3.6   STRING-BASED DISTANCES

The matching coefficient (3.3.5) takes into account how many of the feature vector's strings match literally. There are many other more fine-tuned distance functions, some working on a syntactic character level, for example, the edit distance, and some working on a semantic level, for example, using WordNet, web search engines or ontologies.

   Levenshtein's edit distance transforms one chain $s = (s_1, s_2, \ldots, s_{n^s})$ of n^s symbols $s_i \in S$ into another one t with potentially different length n^t, and is defined as the minimum overall transformation cost that arises through deletions (cost c_d), insertions (cost c_i) and exchanges (cost $c_x \delta(s_j, t_i)$). Computing the minimum cost is normally done via dynamic linear programming that computes an $n^t \times n^s$ matrix c:

   1. $c[0, 0] = 0$
   2. $c[0, j] = j \cdot c_d$ for all $j \in \{1, \ldots, n^s\}$
   3. $c[i, 0] = i \cdot c_i$ for all $i \in \{1, \ldots, n^t\}$
   4. $c[i, j] = \min(c[i - 1, j - 1] + c_x \delta(t_i, s_j), c[i, j - 1] + c_d, c[i - 1, j] + c_i)$
        for all $(i, j) \in \{1, \ldots, n^t\} \times \{1, \ldots, n^s\}$ (small indices first)

The Levenshtein distance between s and t ends up in the matrix element $c[n^t, n^s]$. Figure 3.20 illustrates this process using the strings $s = hello$ and $t = halo$ with an insertion cost of $c_i = 1.01$, a deletion cost of $c_d = 1.1$ and an exchange cost $c_x = 1$ for different letters. The optimal path of operations is marked with arrows from the top left matrix element $c[0, 0]$ to the bottom right matrix element $c[n^t, n^s]$. It involves replacing h with h (cost 0), replacing e with a (cost 1), replacing l with l (cost 0), deleting l (cost 1.1) and replacing o with o (cost 0) totalling a cost of 2.1, which is the smallest possible.

   The algorithm is $O(n^s n^t)$ in time and can be made $O(n^t)$ in memory by observing that the algorithm only ever needs to have access to the preceding matrix row. Levenshtein (1966) introduced a version of this distance for which $c_x = c_i = c_d = 1$ (the so called *edit distance*) in the context of transmitting binary codes over unreliable channels that delete, insert and invert bits. There are

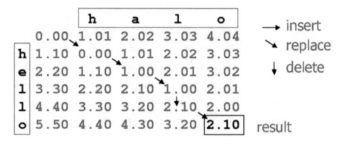

Figure 3.20: Levenshtein distance between *hello* and *halo* with $c_d = 1.1$, $c_i = 1.01$ and $c_x = 1$

generalisations of this algorithm that include transpositions of characters (a common source of typos) and general cost matrices over the set of symbols allowing to assign a smaller cost for easy-to-mix-up letters (for example, c and k or those adjacent on the keyboard).

The Levenshtein distance has particular significance for our difference chain codes from Equation 3.3. The individual symbols of a string have a semantic meaning in that the eight values $0, 1, \ldots, 7$ represent quantised angles $0°, 45°, \ldots, 315°$. Here it makes sense to penalise exchanges depending on how severe the direction encoded in the symbol has changed:

$$c_x(s_j, t_i) = \min((s_j - t_i) \mod 8, (t_i - s_j) \mod 8). \qquad (3.7)$$

This cost of exchange is meant to compute the absolute difference of the angles reflecting the fact that 7 and 0 are neighbouring angles in this quantisation scheme of $45°$.

The *Hamming distance* between two strings of the same length that counts the number of positions at which letters differ can be seen as a trivial case of the Levenshtein distance for which $c_d = c_i = \infty$ and $c_x = 1$.

While the edit distance is purely based on the syntactic form of the words involved, looking at co-occurrence at document level can yield a deeper insight into the semantic similarity of strings. This co-occurrence can be computed from a training set of documents or taken from other external knowledge sources such as the world wide web or the more structured sources that ontologies are. We start by formalising co-occurrence counts.

Let a be a document-word matrix, where each row represents a document in form of a sparse binary word vector. Then

$$b = a^t a$$

is a symmetric matrix, whose element b_{ij} contains the number of documents in which word i co-occurs with word j. a^t denotes the transposed matrix for which $(a^t)_{ij} = a_{ji}$. Each column $b_{i\bullet}$ in the co-occurrence matrix b describes how strongly the word i co-occurs with all the other words of the repository vocabulary. The value

$$d_{\text{co-occ}}(i, j) = 1 - \frac{b_{ij}}{\max(b_{ii}, b_{jj})} \qquad (3.8)$$

is just one possible dissimilarity measure for how far word j is from word i with respect to their joint usage in documents. It changes with the granularity of what is considered to be a document (a window of 10 words, a sentence, a paragraph, a section, a chapter, a book).

One of the biggest resources of word usage is the internet, of which web search engines have indexed several billion web pages as of today. Most search engines tell you in how many web pages a particular word i is mentioned (c_i), and equally in how many web pages two different words i and j both appear (c_{ij}). Gracia and Mena (2008) named the expression

$$d_{\mathrm{nw}}(i, j) = \frac{\max(\log c_i, \log c_j) - \log c_{ij}}{\log N - \min(\log c_i, \log c_j)}$$

the *normalised web distance* between words i and j; here N denotes the number of web pages that this particular web search engine has indexed. d_{nw} was defined earlier by Cilibrasi and Vitányi (2007), who meticulously justified it as an approximation to a normalised information distance. Despite its name d_{nw} violates strict positivity $d_{\mathrm{nw}}(i, j) > 0$ for $i \neq j$: imagine two different words i and j that appear in exactly the same set of web pages; then $c_i = c_j = c_{ij}$ and $d_{\mathrm{nw}}(i, j) = 0$ although $i \neq j$. Even worse, it turns out that d_{nw} violates the triangle inequality, too. As web search engines sometimes return counts that are slightly inconsistent, it can happen in practice that they report numbers with $c_i < c_{ij}$, which will make d_{nw} slightly negative. There may be the additional difficulty to get a reliable estimate for N.

Despite all its shortcomings, d_{nw} is very popular as it gives uncomplicated access to word co-occurrence estimations in a vast corpus. Luckily its definition is scale-invariant, ie, if the number N of indexed web pages multiplies by a factor f, and with it the numbers c_i, c_j and c_{ij}, then the value for $d_{\mathrm{nw}}(i, j)$ stays invariant. However, the world wide web corpus changes over time, and as new words are introduced, phased out or change meaning, their normalised web distances will change, too.

3.4   FEATURE AND DISTANCE STANDARDISATION

If one uses different feature types to describe a multimedia object, then it is desirable that these features are comparable in size. For example, if you had encoded aspects of music in terms of pitch frequency in Hz[6] and beats-per-second, then typical feature vectors would look like $(10,000, 0.8)$. While a difference of 0.2 in the second feature type effects a significant change in perception, a difference of 20 in the first feature type is negligible.

While these differences can be absorbed in the distance functions that work on the features, it is much better to standardise these feature values from the outset. Feature standardisation has two different objectives: one is to make different components of a feature vector that have different origin and meaning comparable in size; the other is to ensure that the size of the feature vector is bounded, and hence distances between two feature vectors. The reason for the second objective is

---

[6]this is only an example: there is something else wrong with using frequency as a feature value in the first place, which is discussed below

that distances between feature vectors are used for result list ranking; if multimedia objects are to be ranked with respect to different features, then it is desirable that their respective distances are in the same range (see fusion section 3.6).

3.4.1 COMPONENT-WISE STANDARDISATION USING CORPUS STATISTICS

For the first objective, features can be standardised component-wise using component mean values and their component-wise mean absolute deviation. Both are computed per component and across the data set. Formally, let v_i^j be the i-th component of the j-th feature vector in a set $F = \{v^1, v^2, \ldots, v^N \in \mathbb{R}^n\}$. This corresponds to the situation where N multimedia objects are indexed with N feature vectors $v^1, v^2, \ldots, v^N \in \mathbb{R}^n$, where each feature vector has n components. The data-set-mean $\overline{v}_i$ of the i-th component of the feature vectors is defined as

$$\overline{v}_i = \frac{1}{N} \sum_{j=1}^{N} v_i^j.$$

Using this value one can compute the mean absolute deviation per component i

$$\overline{s}_i = \frac{1}{N} \sum_{j=1}^{N} |v_i^j - \overline{v}_i|,$$

which amounts to the "typical variation" of the feature component i. Replacing all feature vector components with

$$\tilde{v}_i^j = \frac{v_i^j - \overline{v}_i^j}{s_i}$$

will create feature vectors $\tilde{v}^1, \tilde{v}^2, \ldots, \tilde{v}^N \in \mathbb{R}^n$, whose components have a typical size of 1 and have a mean of 0. This process creates feature vectors with negative components, which most distance measures are oblivious to. Note though, that some distance measures do not allow for negative components, for example, the squared chord distance or probabilistic distance measures. For these it may be better to forgo centring the feature vectors about zero, and

$$\tilde{v}_i^j = v_i^j / s_i$$

will be the far better transformation.

3.4.2 RANGE STANDARDISATION

If the feature components i are known to lie in the range $[a_i, b_i] \ni v_i^j$ each, then the feature vectors can be transformed according to

$$\tilde{v}_i^j = \frac{v_i^j - a_i}{b_i - a_i} \in [0, 1].$$

One can determine suitable values $a_i, b_i \in \mathbb{R}$ easily through

$$a_i = \min_{j=1}^{N} v_i^j \quad \text{and} \quad b_i = \max_{j=1}^{N} v_i^j.$$

This transformation is most useful for uniformly distributed features, but might suffer from the effects of outliers, which adversely move the minimum and maximum boundaries.

3.4.3   RATIO FEATURES

Some feature components are not on a linear scale. For instance, frequency or loudness is perceived on a logarithmic scale. One characteristic of these components is that they are so-called ratio variables for which $1/(k+1)$ and $1/k$ should have the same distance as k and $k+1$. A commonly applied transformation is to work with the logarithm

$$\tilde{v}_i^j = \log(v_i^j)$$

of the variable instead. Ratio features are a special case of features with non-linear response. For example, one might consider using the square root of the file size of an image to approximate its linear size.

3.4.4   VECTOR NORMALISATION

Standardisation makes components of a feature vector comparable in range. This is particularly indicated for feature vectors that have different interpretations or even physical units for different components, but may not be necessary at all in other cases. Even if feature vector components are standardised, there is still the issue that some feature vectors will be typically large (ie, have a large L_p norm) and others will be small. A feature vector that has 100 components, each of which standardised across the data set, is expected to be $\sqrt{10}$ times larger under the Euclidean norm than a component-standardised feature vector with 10 components. Vector normalisation

$$\tilde{v}^j = v^j / L_p(v^j) \tag{3.9}$$

ensures that all the feature vectors have the same L_p norm, which in turn limits the distance of any two such vectors.

An alternative to vector normalisation is distance normalisation, where each vector is divided by a constant c_F that is the average pairwise distance over the feature set F

$$c_F = \frac{1}{|F|^2} \sum_{v_i, v_j \in F} d(v^i, v^j).$$

It is often prohibitive to compute this number, and then a fixed random sample $F' \subset F$ instead of F will give a good estimate for c_F. In any case, scaling the vectors

$$\tilde{v}^j = v^j / c_F \tag{3.10}$$

yields distances of typical feature vector sizes of 1.

It is important to realise that Equation 3.10 *uniformly* scales all vectors by the same factor. If only this particular feature is used for ranking, then the overall ranking will not change. Vector scaling is useful to calibrate relative influence of feature vectors during a fusion of different features. In contrast to this, vector normalisation (3.9) has a *different* effect on different vectors and may well perturb the retrieval results under a particular feature vector, ie, the performance can get better or worse with vector normalisation.

3.5   HIGH-DIMENSIONAL INDEXING

A significant bottleneck when searching any large database for nearest neighbours is the amount of data that needs to be loaded from disk. In traditional relational databases, B-tree or hashing are the predominant disk-based indexing mechanisms for single attributes (dimensions). These approaches are useful for database accesses where each dimension is used independently to select entries. For nearest-neighbour computation *all* dimensions of a feature vector contribute to its distance to the query's feature vector.

It turns out that indexing high-dimensional vectors efficiently is very challenging owing to the *curse of dimensionality*. This term was first used by Bellman (1961)[7] and refers to the phenomenon that our understanding of the space in 2 or 3 dimensions breaks down as the dimensionality of the space increases. Assume for a moment that our feature space is described by a n-dimensional unit hypercube $[0, 1]^n$ containing uniformly distributed data points. Given a query point, how much of the range of each dimension must we consider to capture a proportion p of the data? To enclose a fraction p of the unit volume, the length l in each dimension is $l = p^{1/n}$. If we are trying to enclose only 1% of the data in 10 dimensions, this means we must consider 63% of the range of each dimension, for 100 dimensions this increases to 95% and for 500 dimensions it is 99%. Conversely, 99% of the volume of a 500-dimensional unit hypercube is located in its surface skin of 0.005 thickness! In other words, if we lived in high dimensions we better not peel potatoes as little would be left to eat.

Beyer et al (1999) showed with similar arguments to those above that, as dimensionality increases, all points tend to exhibit the same distance from a query point. This has the ultimate effect of making the nearest neighbour problem ill defined.

Real-world data, such as image features, are unlikely to be uniformly distributed and may exist on a lower-dimensional manifold. This will alleviate some of the symptoms of the curse, however, significant effects for nearest neighbour searching and indexing remain.

It is likely that a real feature space may have an intrinsic dimensionality lower than the apparent data space. Dimensionality reduction methods aim to extract significant information into lower dimensions. Principal component analysis is a common technique, and it is often used in combination with other methods. PCA works well but has drawbacks for indexing. Its complexity

---

[7]illustrating the fact that a Boolean function of n arguments has 2^n cases

can make it impractical for very large datasets with high dimensionality, and there are difficulties with incrementally adding data.

A significant class of methods partition the feature space or data points into tree structures. The first of these for multi-dimensional space was the R-tree developed by Guttman (1984). There have been many variants of this, and they have proved successful in certain circumstances. High-dimensional feature spaces are sparsely populated, and so it becomes hard to partition the data effectively. This is significant for tree-based structures. Indeed, Weber et al (1998) showed that all tree structures are less effective than a linear scan of all data above a certain dimensionality. This led them to develop a vector approximation technique called the VA-file. This accepts the fact that the linear scan is inevitable and attempts to optimise it using compression. They achieve times of 12.5–25% of a linear scan.

Most approaches store and search each dimension of the feature separately. This is often referred to as vertical decomposition, column store or decomposition storage model and gives a very flexible approach as dimensions can be treated differently depending on their significance. For instance, the inverted VA-file of Müller and Henrich (2004) stores each dimension at different quantisation levels and only retrieves at the accuracy needed dependent on the query. The BOND system developed by de Vries et al (2002) uses a branch-and-bound algorithm so that data in later dimensions can be discarded. Finally, Aggarwal and Yu's iGrid (2000) and bitmap indices (Wu et al, 2004a; Sinha and Winslett, 2007) work with vertically decomposed features and use only the part of each dimension close to the query point to generate a similarity value. In the same spirit, Howarth and Rüger (2005c) suggest a new local distance function for only the objects close the query point.

Approximate nearest neighbour approaches relax the constraint of finding exact results to speed up search. Nene and Nayar's method (1997) recovers the best neighbour if it is within ε of the query point. Beis and Lowe (1997) developed a variant of the k-d tree using a best-bin-first algorithm. They used this to efficiently retrieve the nearest or a very close neighbour in a shape indexing context. In a more recent development, Muja and Lowe (2009) published an approach that will take a given dataset and desired degree of precision and automatically determine the best algorithm and parameter values for that. They also describe a new algorithm that applies priority search on hierarchical k-means trees, which they have found to provide a good performance on many datasets. Marius Muja distributes public domain code of their software library called FLANN[8] (Fast Library for Approximate Nearest Neighbours), which implements their ideas.

3.6   FUSION OF FEATURE SPACES AND QUERY RESULTS

3.6.1   SINGLE QUERY EXAMPLE WITH MULTIPLE FEATURES

In this subsection, we assume that there is a single query example q and that each multimedia document m gives rise to a number of low-level features $f_1(m)$, $f_2(m)$, ..., $f_k(m)$, each of which would typically be a vector describing some aspect such as colour, texture, shape, timbre etc.

---

[8]http://people.cs.ubc.ca/~mariusm/index.php/FLANN/FLANN

Combined Overall Distance

Most systems accumulate the distances of these features to the corresponding features of the query q in order to define an overall distance

$$D_w(m, q) = \sum_{i=1}^{r} w_i d_i (f_i(m), f_i(q)) \tag{3.11}$$

between multimedia documents m and a query q. Here $d_i(\cdot, \cdot)$ is a specific distance function between the vectors from the feature i, and $w_i \in \mathbb{R}$ is a weight for the importance of this feature.

Note that the overall distance $D_w(m, q)$ is the number that is used to rank the multimedia documents in the database, and that the ones with the smallest distance to the query are shown to the user as query result, see Figure 3.1. Note also that the overall distance and hence the returned results crucially depend on the weight vector $w = (w_1, \ldots, w_r)$. In most interfaces, the user can either set the weights explicitly as in the interface shown in Figure 4.8, or the system can change the weights implicitly if the user has given feedback on how well the returned documents fit their needs. Section 4.4 covers more on relevance feedback.

Convex Combinations or not?

The weights w_i in Equation 3.11 are arbitrary real numbers, and so is the range of distance functions d_i. Often, however, the distances have been made to be in the same range, and the weights would be restricted to be in the unit interval and to sum to 1:

$$\sum_i w_i = 1 \text{ and } 0 \le w_i \le 1$$

If the weights are restricted in this way then the sum in Equation 3.11 is called a *convex combination*. Some distances are already bounded owing to the nature of the underlying feature vectors (eg, the Manhattan distance between two normalised histograms is always in the range $[0, 2]$) and others can be forced to be bounded through a process called feature standardisation (see Section 3.4). Convex combinations have the clear theoretical advantage that the ensuing overall distance $D_w(m, q)$ will then be bounded in the same way as the $d_i(\cdot, \cdot)$. This might be important if the query consists of multiple query examples, and the distances of these examples are to be fused later. The disadvantage of using convex weight combinations, however, is that they are less expressive. For example, users might want to specify a query by music example requiring that the rhythm and melody of the retrieved music piece should be the same as the query, only the timbre should not be like that at all. In this case, a negative weight for the timbre feature vector would be desirable.

Truncated Result Lists

Taken at face value, Equation 3.11 is incompatible with efficient nearest-neighbour computations in individual feature spaces: for one, the sets of nearest neighbours for the individual features are almost certainly different, and, on the other hand, some features may have a small weight or exhibit a small distance far down their nearest neighbour list for a particular query, so that a large proportion of this particular feature's index data are needed to determine a number, say k, of nearest neighbours with respect to the overall measure $D_w(m, q)$.

One possible way out is to approximate $d_i(f_i(m), f_i(q))$, and hence $D_w(m, q)$, using truncated lists S_i^{gk} of, say, gk nearest neighbours for each individual feature i under $d_i(\cdot, f_i(q))$:

$$\tilde{d}_i(f_i(m), f_i(q)) = \begin{cases} d_i(f_i(m), f_i(q)) & \text{if } m \in S_i^{gk} \\ s_i & \text{otherwise} \end{cases}$$

Here $g \geq 1$ is a multiplier (say, $g = 10$), and s_i is a constant, for instance,

$$s_i = \max_{m \in S_i^{gk}} d_i(f_i(m), f_i(q)).$$

Basically s_i approximates the distance between q and any database object outside S_i^{gk} under feature i. It can be chosen arbitrarily larger to penalise any m that is not in the intersection of S_i^{gk} over i. Under this heuristic, the gk nearest neighbours for each feature i can be determined independently, possibly on different computers. Then there is no need to access the feature vectors of any m that is outside of the truncated lists S_i^{gk}.

CombSum, CombMin and CombMax

Rather than adding distances in Equation 3.11 one can also use the *minimum* of feature distances. Here the smallest distance determines the overall distance thus in effect requiring that *one* of the features be close for overall closeness. Alternatively, one can stipulate that the *maximum* of feature distances determines the overall distance, effectively requiring that *all* of the features be close for overall closeness. These combination mechanisms are also known as *CombSum, CombMin* and *CombMax* and can be extended to work with truncated lists of gk nearest neighbours.

Mc Donald and Smeaton (2005) compare these various fusion mechanisms on the TRECVid (see Subsection 5.4.4) data sets and consistently find that Equation 3.11 is best for combining multiple visual features over a single query. They also find that adding distances (scores) is best for combining a single visual feature over multiple queries.

Merging Individual Ranked Lists

Alternatively, rather than combining individual distances under various features, one can combine the ranked lists of nearest neighbours under the respective features. Rank-based methods largely ignore the feature-induced distances once they have been used to determine the order of multimedia objects. For example, by summing all the ranks that a multimedia object received under various features, one arrives at a new sorting criterion, which is called *Borda count*. It is possible to give preference to certain features using weights resulting in a *weighted Borda count*. Using the minimum of the ranks of a multimedia object with respect to different features corresponds to a *round-robin* method of merging ranks, basically interleaving ranked lists.

Learning Weights in Distance-score Space

Once relevance judgements are available one can ask the question what the best combination strategy is or even deploy machine learning algorithms to automatically determine weights or best fusion strategies (Bartell et al, 1994).

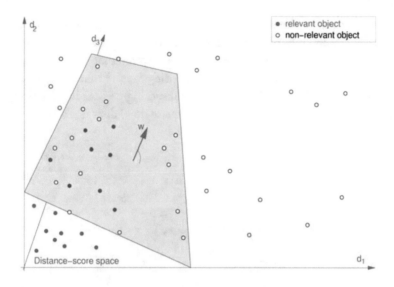

Figure 3.21: Separating relevant from non-relevant distance-score vectors in distance-score space

One way of using relevance judgements to determine an optimal weight vector utilises distances under different feature spaces: each judged object j (ie, a multimedia object where you know whether or not it is relevant to a particular query q), induces a vector $i \mapsto d_i(f_i(j), f(i)q)$ in a r-dimensional *distance-score space* (r is the number of different features). Placing a separating hyperplane between the positive distance-score vectors and the negative distance-score vectors that maximises the margin between these two groups immediately identifies the optimal weight vector for this query: it is a vector perpendicular to the optimal hyperplane. The idealised Figure 3.21 illustrates this property: in this example, clearly Feature 2 is most important to separate relevant from non-relevant vectors, as the separating hyperplane is nearly parallel to the $1 - 3$ plane; the weight vector's 2nd component w_2 is consequently the largest.

In practice, the two sets of vectors will not be clearly separable, as there are bound to be relevant multimedia objects far away from the query and non-relevant ones close by.

3.6.2 MULTIPLE QUERY EXAMPLES

In the case of multiple query examples $q_1, q_2, \ldots, q_s$, it may either be that each example is of a different importance or even that some of the examples are negative examples with the meaning "but the query result should not be anything like these ones". Some of the mechanisms rely on the existence of both positive and negative examples. It is an ungrateful task for any user to come up with negative queries just for the sake of it, so some approaches randomly select examples from a large data set for this purpose assuming they will not be what the user wants.

Single Surrogate Query from Multiple Queries

If the examples are of the same kind (eg, all images or all music), then it is possible to average their respective feature vectors and thus reduce the case to a single surrogate query example. However, this makes the rather restrictive, and arguably unjustified, assumption that relevant database objects form a convex subset in feature space. Convex subsets have the property that averages, or more generally convex combinations, of its elements are still in the subset. Figure 3.22 illustrates why constructing a single surrogate query q from multiple examples (square dots) does not work in general.

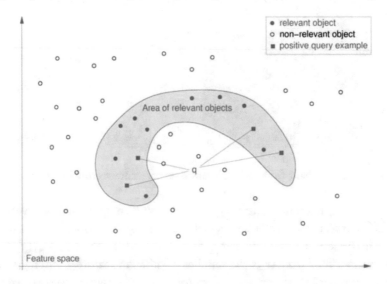

Figure 3.22: Constructing a single query q from multiple examples does not work

Combining Distances from Single Queries

In analogy to Equation 3.11, one can add up — and weight using numbers $u_j \in \mathbb{R}$ — distances brought about by the individual query examples $q_j \in Q$:

$$D^Q(m, Q) = \sum_j u_j D^j(m, q_j) \qquad (3.12)$$

Equation 3.12, which I nickname the parent of all distances, computes the most versatile of all numbers that can be used to sort result lists from a set Q of query examples with positive or negative weights u_j. The distance functions D^j generally will follow Equation 3.11 but can be completely different for each individual query q_j, and involve different feature types, feature weights and distance functions. In analogy with the fusion of features, each $D^j(m, q_j)$ can be computed independently, even on different computers. In the interest of efficiency, the same tricks of using truncated result lists can be deployed here.

Merging Ranked Lists from Single Queries

In the same way as ranked lists from single features can be weighted and merged, this can be done with ranked lists that result from individual query examples, see Subsection 3.6.1 on page 72.

Memory-based Learning

In order to cater for different query examples, each one possibly exhibiting a different desired property, a distance averaging approach as in Equation 3.12 may be as undesirable as creating a single surrogate query as depicted in Figure 3.22.

In this case, intuitively, a better approach would be to reward multimedia objects that are close to any one of the positive query examples. This is what a *distance-weighted k-nearest neighbours approach* (Mitchell, 1997) does. Let Q be the set of query examples of which we know whether they are positive or negative. Q needs to have at least one positive example and one negative example, but we can always pepper Q with unjudged examples from a large set and treat these as negative.

For each of the multimedia objects m that are to be ranked, we compute the set Q^k of m's k nearest neighbours in Q and determine the subsets $P, N \subset Q^k$ of positive and negative examples, respectively. Naturally, we have $|P| + |Q| = k$. The number

$$R(m) = \frac{\sum_{p \in P} \left(D^p(m, p) + \varepsilon\right)^{-1}}{\sum_{n \in N} \left(D^n(m, n) + \varepsilon\right)^{-1} + \varepsilon},$$

where ε is a small positive number to avoid division by zero, determines how the multimedia objects should be sorted, given the query set Q.

Note that in this application, we compute nearest neighbour lists in the set of query examples (of an arbitrary m in the repository), while before we have always computed nearest neighbours in the full repository (of a query example). Although this way of combining evidence from a set Q of query examples has been shown to give better results than the combination of distances (Pickering and Rüger, 2003), it is rather resource-consuming. For large multimedia repositories, it may only be feasible to use the distance-weighted k-nearest neighbours approach for re-ranking candidate subsets rather than for ranking the full repository.

3.6.3 ORDER OF FUSION

Rather a lot of evidence has gone into the similarity ranking block of the simple diagram in Figure 3.1: distances with respect to many different feature vector types and distances with respect to different query examples. Above subsections seem to be suggesting that one should fuse first wrt features and then wrt query examples. In fact, this could be the other way round or with a flat structure where all the evidence is combined at the same time. If one uses the parent of all distances, Equation 3.12, then it does not matter as nested finite sums commute:

$$
\begin{aligned}
D^Q(m, Q) &= \sum_j u_j \sum_i w_i d_i^j (f_i^j(m), f_i^j(q_j)) \\
&= \sum_i w_i \sum_j u_j d_i^j (f_i^j(m), f_i^j(q_j)) \\
&= \sum_{i,j} w_i u_j d_i^j (f_i^j(m), f_i^j(q_j))
\end{aligned}
$$

If each step is approximated through truncated ranked lists — or merged, normalised, standardised, combined or machine-learned in a non-linear way otherwise — then the order of these processes will have an effect on the overall ranking.

3.7   EXERCISES

3.7.1   COLOUR HISTOGRAMS

Colour is perceived as a point (r, g, b) in a *three-dimensional* space. Each colour component (red, green and blue) is usually encoded as an integer between 0 and 255 (1 byte); there are two principal methods to create colour histograms: you can compute three 1d histograms of each of the r, g and b components independently or you can compute one 3d colour histogram.

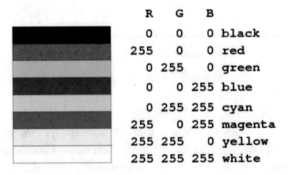

R	G	B	
0	0	0	black
255	0	0	red
0	255	0	green
0	0	255	blue
0	255	255	cyan
255	0	255	magenta
255	255	0	yellow
255	255	255	white

Figure 3.23: A striped colour test image

(a) If you divide each of the red, green and blue axes into n_r, n_g, n_b equal intervals, respectively, then the 3d colour cube $[0, 255]^3$ is subdivided into $n_r n_g n_b$ cuboids or bins. Show that by mapping (r, g, b) to

$$
\left\lfloor \frac{n_r r}{256} \right\rfloor n_g n_b + \left\lfloor \frac{n_g g}{256} \right\rfloor n_b + \left\lfloor \frac{n_b b}{256} \right\rfloor
$$

you get an enumeration scheme $0, \ldots, n_r n_g n_b - 1$ for the cuboids. A 3d colour histogram of an image is a *list of the numbers of the pixels in an image that fall into each of the different cuboids* in colour space. In other words, you look at each pixel in an image, compute above index from its colour (r, g, b) and increment the corresponding variable, which records the number of pixels that fall into this colour cuboid.

(b) Compute both types of colour histograms for the image in Figure 3.23 (the colours of the stripes are given by the table next to the image). Use $64 = 4^3$ bin cubes for the 3d-bin-histogram and 22 bins for each of the three colour-component histograms (yielding 66 bins altogether), so that both histogram types have a similar number of bins.

(c) Using the same visualisation method for 3d colour histograms as demonstrated in Section 3.2 yields Figure 3.24. Why are the colours in the visualisation different from the original colours of the image?

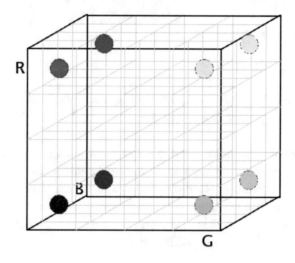

Figure 3.24: 3d colour histogram for the striped colour test image

Visualise the three 1d histograms of the r, g and b components that you computed in (b). Given these histograms which colours might have appeared in the original image?

Which of the two colour histogram methods has retained more information about the colour distribution in the original picture? How did it come about that one of the two methods lost vital information despite having roughly the same number of bins (64 vs 66)?

3.7.2 HSV COLOUR SPACE QUANTISATION

The HSV colour space is popular because it separates the pure colour aspects from brightness. Figure 3.25 visualises the aspects of hue (H) that corresponds to a spectral frequency, saturation (S) that expresses how pure the colour is, and value (V) that expresses the apparent brightness of a colour. The hue values H are arranged on a circle and encoded from $0\,°$ to $360\,°$, which is again the same as 0°. Zero saturation S means that the colour is grey and the higher the saturation is the less grey is mixed into it up to a value of 100% where the colour is deemed to represent a single spectral frequency, ie, a rainbow colour. H and S are polar coordinates where H is an angle and S is the radius. The pair (H, S) describes the chromaticity of a colour, while its apparent brightness V is independent from chromaticity. One other advantage of HSV over RGB is that it appears more intuitive to talk about colours in terms of their brightness and spectral names rather than the mixture coefficients of R, G and B.

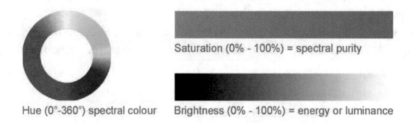

Figure 3.25: HSV coordinates

Show that all possible (H, S, V) values make up a cylinder and that the grey values reside on the central axis of the cylinder. Show that the conversion between RGB and HSV cannot be continuous.

One natural way of subdividing the HSV space into bins is to subdivide each coordinate linearly. Which of the so created *different* HSV bins will contain colour representations that are almost certainly in one single bin in RGB space (this is the effect of above discontinuity)? Which bins in HSV space do you need to merge, so that this discontinuity is no longer visible?

How would you need to subdivide HSV space so that its bins have the same volume as the set of points in RGB space that are mapped into them?

3.7.3   CIE LUV COLOUR SPACE QUANTISATION

CIE[9] LUV (International Commission on Illumination, 1986) describes the physical appearance of colour, independent of the reproduction device, using the idea of a human standard observer. This colour space strives to be perceptually uniform in the sense that the Euclidean distance between any two points in colour space should resemble the human perception of the grade of colour difference. As a consequence, the transformation from RGB to CIE LUV is highly non-linear and the resulting colour space is not of a simple geometric form: Figure 3.26 depicts the chromaticity plane of CIE LUV. How should the CIE LUV colour space be quantised?

---

[9]http://cie.co.at — Commission internationale de l'éclairage

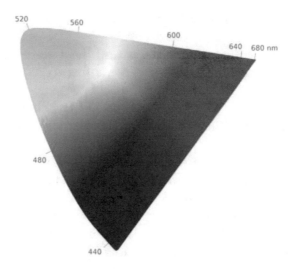

Figure 3.26: Chromaticity plane of the CIE LUV colour space

3.7.4 SKEWNESS AND KURTOSIS

The third and fourth central moments are used to define skewness and kurtosis: skewness is defined as

$$s = \overline{p}_3 / \sqrt{\overline{p}_2}^3 ,$$

while kurtosis is defined as

$$k = \overline{p}_4 / \overline{p}_2^2 - 3.$$

Verify that subtracting 3 in the definition above makes the kurtosis of any normal distribution zero irrespective of its parameters. Show that the above definitions of skewness and kurtosis are dimensionless (ie, if the underlying quantity $p(i, j)$ had a physical dimension then s and k do not) and scale invariant (ie, if the underlying quantity was multiplied by a constant c then the values of s and c are not affected by this). Think of a way to define general standardised central moments that are dimensionless and scale invariant and compare with a textbook definition of standardised central moments (the textbook definition of the second standardised central moment is always 1). Note that Equation 3.2 is neither dimensionless nor scale invariant — instead its aim is to generate values that are on the same scale.

3.7.5 BOUNDARIES FOR TAMURA FEATURES

Determine the exact areas of an image in which coarseness, contrast and directionality can be determined, see Figure 3.6.

3.7.6   DISTANCES AND DISSIMILARITIES

Show that the Bray-Curtis dissimilarity and the squared chord dissimilarity violate the triangle inequality, while the Canberra distance is a true distance, ie, that $d(v, w) = d(w, v), d(v, w) = 0$ if and only if $v = w$ and $d(x, z) \leq d(x, y) + d(y, z)$.

Show that the Manhattan distance and the partial histogram intersection are equivalent, ie, lead to the same ordering if the feature vectors are normalised with respect to the L_1 norm and non-negative.

Show that the Euclidean distance and the cosine dissimilarity are equivalent, ie, lead to the same ordering if the feature vectors are normalised with respect to the L_2 norm and non-negative.

Draw the unit balls B_p in $\mathbb{R}^2$ with respect to the Minkowski norm L_p for $p \in \{0.5, 1, 2, \infty\}$. The formal definition is $B_p = \{x \in \mathbb{R}^2 \mid L_p(x) \leq 1\}$. Show that $B_{0.5}$ is *not* convex, ie, points on a straight line between 2 points within $B_{0.5}$ are not necessarily in $B_{0.5}$. Show that, as a consequence, $L_{0.5}$ violates the triangle inequality, ie, it does not induce a distance. Show that L_p induces a distance for $p \geq 1$.

3.7.7   ORDINAL DISTANCES — PEN-PAL MATCHING

The table below shows a number of people's favourite writer, travel destination, colour, newspaper, city, genre and means of communication. Work out who would make the best pair of pen-pals. Which pair would be least compatible?

Ally	V Woolf	UK	red	Guardian	London	crime	twitter
Bert	L Carroll	Canada	green	Times	Tokyo	poetry	sms
Cris	L Carroll	Italy	green	Times	NY	drama	sms
Doro	V Woolf	Spain	blue	Mirror	London	fiction	e-mail
Enzo	V Woolf	Canada	green	Observer	Tokyo	drama	sms
Fred	M Proust	Spain	green	Mirror	London	crime	twitter

3.7.8   ASYMMETRIC BINARY FEATURES

The table below shows a number of people's gender and character traits. Each of the traits occurs rather infrequently in the population (ie, they are *asymmetric* binary features: P = present, N = not present). Ignoring the gender, work out who would make the best pair of pen-pals. Which pair would be least compatible?

Name	gender	character					
Ally	F	N	P	N	N	N	N
Bert	M	N	P	P	N	N	N
Cris	F	P	P	P	N	P	P
Doro	F	P	N	N	P	N	N
Enzo	M	P	P	N	P	P	P
Fred	M	P	N	P	P	P	P

3.7.9   JACCARD DISTANCE

Show that definition (3.3.5) for the Jaccard distance is identical to the definition (2.3) for resemblance when applied to sparse vector encodings of bags of words.

Write the matching coefficient (3.3.5) in terms of c_{xy} as in (2.4) and discuss the difference to the Jaccard distance.

3.7.10   LEVENSHTEIN DISTANCE

It is easy to see that the general Levenshtein distance violates the symmetry requirement $d_L(s, t) = d_L(t, s)$ if the cost of deletion differs from the cost of insertion. However, prove that the edit distance is a proper metric, where the cost of deletion, the cost of insertion and the cost of exchanging different symbols are all 1.

3.7.11   CO-OCCURRENCE DISSIMILARITY

Compute the co-occurrence for the document word matrix of the "Humpty Dumpty" nursery rhyme on page 35. In this setting, what are the distances between *humpty* and *dumpty*, and between *king* and *horse*? What would change if Equation 3.8 used min instead of max in the denominator?

3.7.12   CHAIN CODES AND EDIT DISTANCE

Encode the pixel boundary of a 4×4 square and of a 3×5 rectangle as difference chain codes and compute their edit distance.

3.7.13   TIME WARPING DISTANCE

Modify the Levenshtein distance for difference chain codes such that local stretching can happen at no cost. Your solution should be scale invariant, for instance,

$$d_{Ldcc}(123, 111223333) = 0.$$

Figure 3.27 gives you an idea how this distance could be processed in the case of the two strings 000710 and 01700000020, but your solution may well look different.

```
        0 1 7 0 0 0 0 0 2 0
     0  - - - - - - - - - - -
  0  -  0 1 2 2 2 2 2 2 4 4      0170000020
  0  -  0 1 2 2 2 2 2 2 4 4
  0  -  0 1 2 2 2 2 2 2 4 4      000710
  7  -  1 2 1 2 3 3 3 3 5 5
  1  -  2 1 3 2 3 4 4 4 4 5
  0  -  2 2 2 2 2 2 2 2 4 4   result = 4
```

Figure 3.27: Time warping distance between curves represented by difference chain codes

3.7.14 FEATURE STANDARDISATION

Assume you have six feature vectors of the kind (age [year], height [m]) as follows: $v^1 = (10, 1.30)$, $v^2 = (20, 1.70)$, $v^3 = (30, 1.60)$, $v^4 = (40, 1.80)$, $v^5 = (50, 1.70)$ and $v^6 = (60, 9.90)$. Note that the last vector contains a deliberate outlier.

Compute standardised feature vectors according to Subsection 3.4.1.

s_i is a "typical range" of the component i; sometimes the *empirical standard deviation*

$$\sigma_i = \sqrt{\frac{1}{N-1} \sum_j (v_i^j - \bar{v}_i)^2}$$

is used instead of s_i. In our case, $\sigma_1 = 18.7$ and $\sigma_2 = 3.38$ (rounded); argue why the standard deviation is more susceptible to the outlier of 9.90m height than the mean absolute deviation.

One could also use the *median* absolute deviation (defined as the middle-ranked value of all the absolute deviations sorted by size) instead of the mean absolute deviation. How would this affect the standardisation process in the presence of outliers. How about using the median instead of the mean (component-wise)?

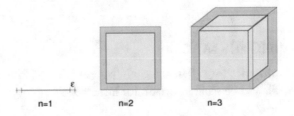

Figure 3.28: Skin of a cube in different dimensions

3.7.15 CURSE OF DIMENSIONALITY

Consider an n-dimensional feature space with a query vector at $q = 0$ and a hypercube $H_n = [-1, 1]^n$ of volume 2^n around it. Assume the hypercube contains uniformly distributed vectors, ie, each component is independently and identically distributed with a random uniform distribution in the range of $[-1, 1]$. The skin S_n^ε of H_n with thickness ε is defined as

$$S_n^\varepsilon = H_n \setminus [-1 + \varepsilon, 1 - \varepsilon]^n,$$

ie, it contains all points $x \in H_n$ that have at least one component x_i close to the boundary of the interval $[-1, 1]$, see Figure 3.28.

What is the probability that a randomly chosen vector of H_n lies in the skin S_n^ε? Plot this probability as a function of n for $\varepsilon = 0.01$. Show that the maximum distance (induced by the maximum norm L_∞, see Subsection 3.3.1) of q to any point s in the skin S_n^ε is bounded by

$$1 - \varepsilon \le d_\infty(q, s) \le 1,$$

ie, nearly every point in H_n has a distance to q of nearly 1.

3.7.16 IMAGE SEARCH

Sketch the block diagram of a colour-and-texture-based image search engine for curtain fabrics. Explain the general workings of a content-based search engine and contrast it with the workings of a text search engine in terms of retrieval and indexing technology.

CHAPTER 4

Added Services

4.1 VIDEO SUMMARIES

Even if the challenges of the previous section were all solved and if the automated methods of Chapters 2 and 3 enabled a retrieval process with high precision (proportion of the retrieved items that are relevant) and high recall (proportion of the relevant items that are retrieved), it would still be vital to present the retrieval results in a way so that the users can quickly decide to which degree those items are relevant to them.

Images are most naturally displayed as thumbnails, and their relevance can quickly be judged by users. Presenting and summarising videos is a bit more involved. The main metaphor used for this is that of a *storyboard* that contains *keyframes* with some text about the video. Several systems exist that summarise news stories in this way, most notably Informedia (Christel et al, 1999) and Físchlár (Smeaton et al, 2004). The Informedia system devotes much effort to added services such as face recognition and speaker voice identification allowing retrieval of the appearance of known people. Informedia also provides alternative modes of presentation, eg, through film skims or by assembling 'collages' of images, text and other information (eg, maps) sourced via references from the text (Christel and Warmack, 2001). Físchlár's added value lies in the ability to personalise the content (with the user expressing like or dislike of stories) and in assembling lists of related stories and recommendations. Sheffield University's Rich News system automatically annotates radio and television news with the aid of resources retrieved from the world wide web by combining automatic speech recognition with information extraction techniques (Dowman et al, 2005).

Our very own TV news search engine ANSES (Pickering et al, 2003) records the main BBC evening news along with the sub-titles, indexes them, breaks the video stream into shots (defined as those video sequences that are generated during a continuous operation of the camera), extracts one key-frame per shot, automatically glues shots together to form news stories based on an overlap in vocabulary in the sub-titles of adjacent shots (using lexical chains), and assembles a story-board for each story. Stories can be browsed or retrieved via text searches. Figure 4.1 shows the interface of ANSES. We use the natural language toolset GATE (Cunningham, 2002) for automated discovery of organisations, people, places and dates; displaying these prominently as part of a storyboard as in Figure 4.1 provides an instant indication of what the news story is about. ANSES also displays a short automated textual extraction summary, again using lexical chains to identify the most salient sentences. These summaries are never as informative as hand-made ones, but users of the system have found them crucial for judging whether or not they are interested in a particular returned search result.

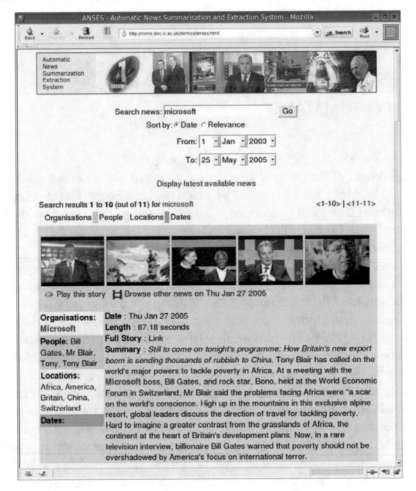

Figure 4.1: News search engine interface

Dissecting the video stream into shots and associating one keyframe along with text from subtitles to each shot has another advantage: a video collection can essentially be treated as an image collection, where each, possibly annotated, image acts as entry point into the video.

At this point, I would like to show how features from video frames can be used to split videos into shots, ie, the segments that were used to edit the movie. Normally the change from one shot to another would be either an abrupt change (a cut), or a gradual change, for example, by fading in and out. In order to detect shots, it is useful to compare neighbouring frames to see whether they are significantly different. For gradual transitions, it may be useful to additionally compare frames that are further apart (say, 4, 8 and 16 frames). I will demonstrate this technique with a short movie that was made by Vlad Tanasescu, a PhD student at KMi. The movie is a science fiction trailer. First I invite you to watch the video by clicking on Figure 4.2 (or via `http://people.kmi.open.ac.uk/stefan/mir-book/Anticipation.mpg`).

Figure 4.2: Sohan Jheeta in *Anticipation*, a video by Vlad Tanasescu (click frame to play)

This video stream is decomposed into single frames, and each frame is subdivided into a 3x3 grid of tiles. For each tile we compute a straightforward 3d colour histogram as in Figure 3.3. Then we define the distance between any two frames as the median of the distances between corresponding tiles. This has the effect of ignoring large changes in some tiles brought about by camera or object movement rather than a change to a different scene. An averaging difference measure at time t n frames apart (but also averaged over n frames) is defined as follows:

$$d_n(t) = \frac{1}{n} \sum_{i=0}^{n-1} d^f(t+i, t-n+i), \qquad (4.1)$$

where $d^f(i, j)$ represents the median block distance between frames i and j.

If the distance function d_2 between two adjacent frames, between frames 4 frames apart (d_4) and between 8 frames (d_8) peaks at the same frame, and the peaks are above a certain threshold, then a cut boundary is called. Gradual transitions are detected through coinciding peaks of d_8 and d_{16} above another threshold. These two thresholds can be set via a test set of known videos in order to adapt them to the type of material. Rapidly changing MTV movies will need other thresholds than, say, the famously long scenes in a typical movie of the Russian director Tarkovsky. The video of Figure 4.3 (or directly from `http://people.kmi.open.ac.uk/stefan/mir-book/anticipation-processed-2.mpg`) visualises the process by plotting the distances d_2, d_4, d_8 and d_{16}. The top row indicates a cut via a | line and a gradual transition with a V sign. The movie itself is played at double speed, while the 3d texture false colour feature and the direct 3d colour histogram of the full frame are displayed for further illustration (though neither of these are directly used by our video shot boundary detection algorithm).

The shot boundary detection problem has attracted much attention as it is an essential pre-processing step to virtually all video analysis. Smeaton et al (2009a) give an overview of the TRECVid shot boundary detection task summarising the most significant of the approaches taken over the years from 2001 to 2007.

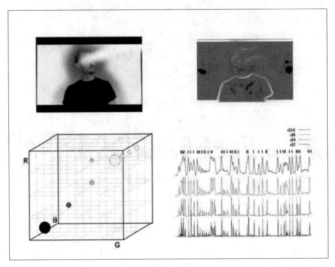

Figure 4.3: Processing a video to detect shot boundaries (click frame for video)

This analysis gives rise to creating *keyframes* from the video shots, which give a clear automated visual summary. Although there are sophisticated algorithms to identify the "best" frame from a shot (eg, by considering the blurriness of an image, the size of dominating objects, variance of parameters etc), we use the 10th frame into a shot for simplicity and in order to avoid overlaid frames that tend to be present at the beginning or end of shots with gradual transitions. Figure 4.4 shows the keyframes from our automated process.

4.2   PARADIGMS IN INFORMATION VISUALISATION

The last decade has witnessed an explosion in interest in the field of information visualisation, (Hemmje et al, 1994; Ankerst et al, 1996; Card, 1996; Shneiderman et al, 2000; Börner, 2000; Keim et al, 2004). Here we present three visualisation paradigms, based on our earlier design studies (Au et al, 2000; Carey et al, 2003). These techniques all revolve around a representation of documents in the form of bag-of-words vectors, which can be clustered to form groups. We use a variant of the buckshot clustering algorithm for this. Basically, the top, say, 100 documents that were returned from a query are clustered via hierarchical clustering to initialise document centroids for k-means clustering that puts all documents returned by a query into groups. Another common element of

Figure 4.4: Keyframes summary of *Anticipation*

our visualisations is the notion of *keywords* that are specific to the returned set of documents. The keywords are computed using a simple statistic; for details see (Carey et al, 2003). A few visualisation methods are described in the following subsections.

Sammon Cluster View

This paradigm uses a Sammon map to generate a two-dimensional screen location from a many-dimensional vector representing a cluster centroid. This map is computed using an iterative gradient search (Sammon, 1969) while attempting to preserve the pairwise distances between the cluster centres. Clusters are thus arranged so that their mutual distances are indicative of their relationship. The idea is to create a visual landscape for navigation. Figure 4.5 shows an example of such an interface. The display has three panels, a scrolling table panel to the left, a graphic panel in the middle and a scrolling text panel to the right that contains the traditional list of returned documents as hotlinks and snippets. In the graphic panel, each cluster is represented by a circle and is labelled with its two most frequent keywords. The radius of the circle represents the cluster size. The distance between any two circles in the graphic panel is an indication of the similarity of their respective clusters - the nearer the clusters, the more likely the documents contained within will be similar. When the mouse passes over the cluster circle, a tool-tip box in the form of a pop-up menu appears that allows the user to select clusters and *drill down*, ie, re-cluster and re-display only the documents in the selected clusters. The back button undoes this process and climbs the hierarchy (*drill up*). The table of keywords includes box fields that can be selected. At the bottom of the table is a filter button that makes the scrolling text window display only the hot-links and snippets from documents that contain the selected keywords.

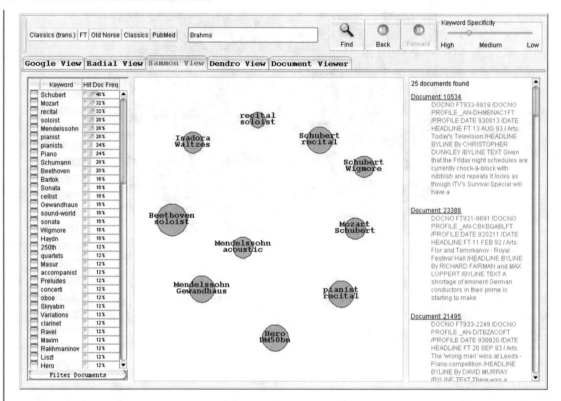

Figure 4.5: Sammon map for cluster-guided search

Dendro Map Visualisation

The Dendro Map visualisation represents documents as leaf nodes of a binary tree that is output by the buckshot clustering algorithm, see Figure 4.6. With its plane-spanning property and progressive shortening of branches towards the periphery, the Dendro Map mimics the result of a non-Euclidean transformation of the plane as used in hyperbolic maps without suffering from their computational load. Owing to spatial constraints, the visualisation depth is confined to five levels of the hierarchy with nodes of the lowest level representing either documents or subclusters. Different colours facilitate visual discrimination between individual documents and clusters. Each lowest level node is labelled with the most frequent keyword of the subcluster or document. This forms a key component of the Dendro Map as it gives the user the cues needed for navigating through the tree. As the user moves the mouse pointer over an internal node, the internal nodes and branches of the associated subcluster change colour from light blue to dark blue while the leaf nodes, ie, document representations, turn bright red. As in the Sammon Map, a tool-tip window provides additional information about the cluster and can be used to display a table with a list of keywords associated with the cluster. The user may drill down on any internal node. The selected node will as a result

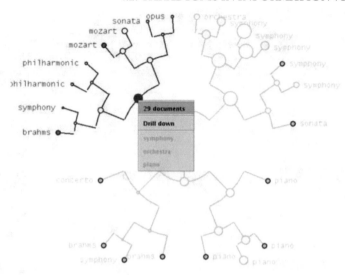

Figure 4.6: Dendro Map - A plane-spanning binary tree (query "Beethoven")

replace the current root node at the center and the entire display is re-organized around the new root. The multi-level approach of the Dendro Map allows the user to gain a quick overview over the document collection and to identify promising subsets.

Radial Interactive Visualisation

Radial (Figure 4.7) is similar to VIBE (Korfhage, 1991), to Radviz (Hoffman et al, 1999) and to Lyberworld (Hemmje et al, 1994). It places the keyword nodes round a circle, and the position of the document dots in the middle depend on the force of invisible springs connecting them to keyword nodes: the more relevant a keyword for a particular document, the stronger its spring pulls on the document. Hence, we make direct use of the bag-of-words representation without explicit clustering. Initially, the twelve highest ranking keywords are displayed in a circle. The interface lets the user move the keywords, and the corresponding documents follow this movement. This allows the user to manually cluster the documents based on the keywords they are interested in. As the mouse passes over the documents, a bubble displays a descriptive piece of text. The location of document dots is not unique owing to dimensionality reduction, and there may be many reasons for a document to have a particular position. To mitigate this ambiguity in Radial, the user can click on a document dot, and the keywords that affect the location of document are highlighted. A choice of keywords used in the display can be exercised by clicking on two visible lists of words. Zoom buttons allow the degree of projection to be increased or reduced so as to distinguish between documents around the edges of the display or at the centre. The Radial visualisation appears to be a good interactive tool to structure the document set according to one's own preferences by shifting keywords around in the display.

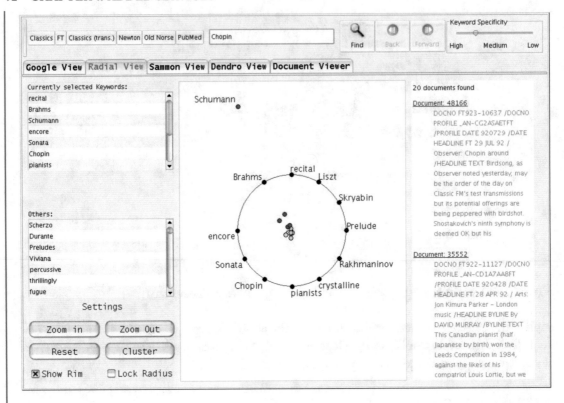

Figure 4.7: Radial Visualisation

Unified Approach

The integration of the paradigms into one application offers the possibility of browsing the same result set in several different ways simultaneously. The cluster-based visualisations give a broader overall picture of the result, while the Radial visualisation allows the user to focus on subsets of keywords. Also, as the clusters are approximations that highlight particular keywords, it may be useful to return to the Radial visualisation and examine the effect of these keywords upon the whole document set. The Radial visualisation will perhaps be more fruitful if the initial keywords match the user's area of interest. The Sammon Map will let the user dissect search sets and re-cluster subsets, gradually homing in on target sets. This interface was developed within the joint NSF-EC project CHLT[1]; it was evaluated from a human-computer-interaction point of view with encouraging results (Chawda et al, 2005) and has proven useful in real-world multi-lingual scholarly collections (Rydberg-Cox et al, 2004).

---

[1]http://www.chlt.org

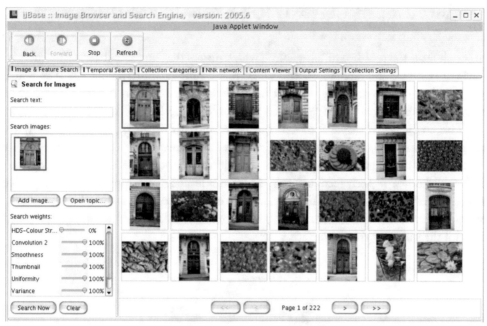

(a) Query by example (left panel) with initial results in the right panel

(b) A new query made of three images from (a) results in many more dark-door images

Figure 4.8: Visual search for images of dark doors starting with a bright-door example

4.3   VISUAL SEARCH AND RELEVANCE FEEDBACK

Implicit and Explicit Relevance Feedback

Visual search faces the problem of "polysemy", which means that images submitted as query (rather than words) normally are ambiguous and allow many different interpretations. It is widely acknowledged that visual search engines that incorporate feedback from the user either by explicitly rating suggested first results or gathered implicitly, eg, by looking at the user's behaviour or actions. This so called relevance feedback has been, and still is, in the centre of many studies: Heesch and Rüger (2003) evaluated a specific *explicit* relevance feedback mechanism for image-retrieval, while White et al (2004) deployed a simulation-centric evaluation methodology to measure how well known *implicit* feedback models learn relevance and improve search effectiveness. Following this White et al (2006) later developed an implicit feedback approach for interactive Information Retrieval. Hopfgartner et al (2007) model implicit information for interpreting the user's actions with the search engine's interface.

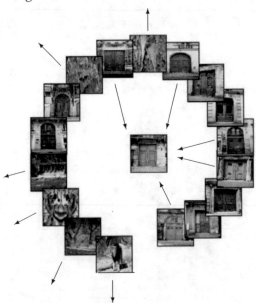

Figure 4.9: A relevance feedback model

Ruthven et al (2003) present five user experiments on incorporating behavioral information into the relevance feedback process in information retrieval, concentrating on ranking terms for query expansion and selecting new terms to add to the user's query. Oyekoya and Stentiford (2004) have proposed one particularly interesting device for implicit feedback during the image search process: an eye-tracking device. Their use for visual search was studied by Yang et al (2002) in terms of psychophysical models. Clough and Sanderson (2004) simulated user interaction with a cross-lingual image retrieval system, and in particular the situation in which a user selects one or more relevant images from the top n; using textual captions associated with the images, relevant images are used to create a feedback model in the Lemur language model for information retrieval, and they show that feedback is beneficial, even when only one relevant document is selected.

Query Point vs Weight Space Moving

The visual query-by-example paradigm discussed in Chapter 2 gives rise to relatively straightforward interfaces; an image is dragged into a query box, or, eg, specified via a URL, and the best matching images are displayed in a ranked list to be inspected by the user, see Figure 4.8(a). A natural extension of such an interface is to offer the selection of relevant results as new query elements. This type of relevance feedback, a.k.a. *query point moving*, is shown in Figure 4.8(b).

One other main type of relevance feedback, *weight space movement*, assumes that the relative weight of the multitude of features that one can assign to images (eg, structured metadata fields such as author, creation date and location; low-level visual features such as colour, shape, structure and texture; free-form text) can be learned from user feedback. Of the methods mentioned in Chapter 2, our group chose analytic weight updating as this has a very small execution time. The idea is that users can specify the degree to which a returned image is relevant to their information needs. This is done by having a visual representation; the returned images are listed in a spiral, and the distance of an image to the centre of the screen is a measure of the relevance that the search engine assigns to a specific image. Users can now move the images around with the mouse or place them in the centre with a left mouse click and far away with a right click. Figure 4.9 shows this relevance feedback model. We evaluated the effectiveness of negative feedback, positive feedback and query point moving, and found that combining the latter two yields the biggest improvement in terms of mean average precision (Heesch and Rüger, 2003).

4 Factor Interaction Model

Liu et al (2009c) propose a visual content-based image retrieval system - uInteract (see Figure 4.10), which is a relevance feedback system based on a four-factor user interaction model based on relevance region, relevance level, time and frequency (Liu et al, 2009b). This system focuses on improving the user interaction. The key features of the visual interface are:

(1) The query image panel is a browsing panel. The user browses the query panel and selects one or more images from the provided query images as initial query image(s) to start the search with.

(2) Users can provide both positive and negative examples to a search query, and further expand or reformulate the query. This is a way to deliver the 'relevance region' factor.

(3) By allowing the user to override the automatically generated ranking (integer 1-20) of positive and negative query images, we enable the user to directly influence the importance level of the feedback. The optional 'relevance level' factor is generated by the ranking functionality.

(4) The display of the results in the interface takes a search-based linear display format but with the addition of showing not only the best matches but also the worst matches. This functionality aims to enable users to control the model directly.

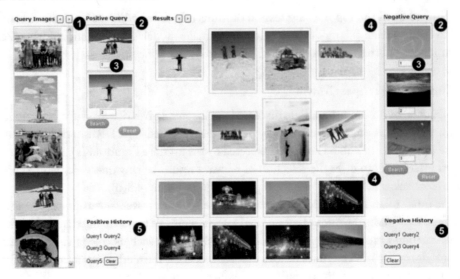

Figure 4.10: The uInteract interface

(5) The query history not only provides users with the ability to reuse their previous queries, but it also enables them to expand future search queries by taking previous queries into account. The positive and negative history panels together with the current query feed the 'time' and 'frequency' factor of the four-factor user interaction model.

Social Context

A new and relatively unexplored area of relevance feedback is the exploitation of social context information. By looking not only at the behaviour and attributes of the user, but also his past interactions and also the interactions of people he has some form of social connection with could yield useful information when determining whether search results are relevant or not. Browsing systems could recommend data items based on the actions of a social network instead of just a single user, using more data to yield better results.

The use of such social information is also becoming important for multimedia meta data generation, particular in the area of folksonomies where the feedback of users actively produces the terms and taxonomies used to describe the media in the system instead of using a predetermined, prescribed dictionary (Voss, 2007). This can be seen being effectively used in online multimedia systems such as Flickr[2] and del.icio.us[3].

---

[2]http://www.flickr.com
[3]http://del.icio.us

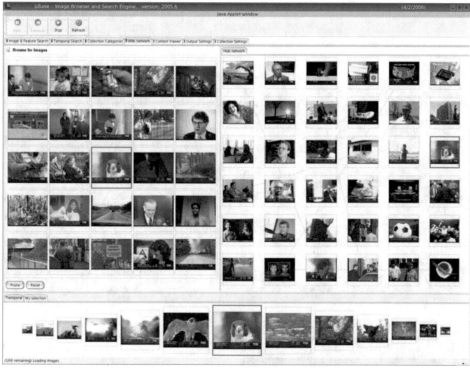

(a) Initial visual summary of the database (right panel) from which the user chooses the falcon, its nearest lateral neighbours are then displayed in the left panel

(b) Clicking on any image will make it the centre of the nearest neighbours panel and display its associated lateral neighbours around it

Figure 4.11: Lateral browsing for an image "from behind the pitcher in a baseball game. . ."

Starting with the football image (upper left) from the database overview, one of its lateral neighbours is an image of a lawn with a sprinkler; when this is made the focal image (upper right), there are already images from baseball scenes. Clicking on one of them (lower left) reveals that there are more of this kind; they can be enlarged and the corresponding video played in the "viewer tab" (lower right).

Figure 4.12: Alternative ways to browse for images "from behind the pitcher ..."

4.4   BROWSING

Some of the research puts the user in the loop to facilitate the bridging of the semantic gap that is inherent in machine-interpretations of audio-visual media: some of this is covered by the notion of relevance feedback in the previous section. In this section, I cover research on alternative resource discovery methods — these focus mainly on browsing and the presentation of the results of the resource discovery mission, be it from searching or browsing.

The idea of representing text documents in a nearest-neighbour network was first presented by Croft and Parenty (1985), albeit, as an internal representation of the relationships between documents and terms, not for browsing. Document networks for interactive browsing were identified by Cox (1992, 1995). Attempts to introduce the idea of browsing into content-based image retrieval include Santini and Jain's *El niño* system (2000) attempt to combine query-based search with browsing. The system tries to display configurations of images in feature space such that the mutual distances between images are preserved as well as possible. Feedback is given in the same spirit as in Figure 4.9 by manually forming clusters of images that appear similar to the user. This in turn results in an altered configuration with potentially new images being displayed. Urban et al (2006) is another example of introducing browsing for image discovery; their work is based on Campbell's (2000) ostensive model that retains the basic mode of query based retrieval but in addition allows browsing through a dynamically created local tree structure.

Other network structures that have increasingly been used for information visualisation and browsing are Pathfinder networks (Dearholt and Schvaneveldt, 1990). They are constructed by removing redundant edges from a potentially much more complex network. Fowler et al (1992) use Pathfinder networks to structure the relationships between terms from document abstracts, between document terms and between entire documents. The user interface supports access to the browsing structure through prominently marked high-connectivity nodes.

Our group (Heesch and Rüger, 2004) determines the nearest neighbour for the image under consideration (which we call the *focal* image) for *every* combination of features. This results in a set of what we call *lateral neighbours*. By calculating the lateral neighbours of all database images, we generate a network that lends itself to browsing. Lateral neighbours share some properties of the focal image, but not necessarily all. For example, a lateral neighbour may share text annotations with the focal image, but no visual similarity with it at all, or it may have a very similar colour distribution, but no structural similarity, or it may be similar in all features except shape, etc. As a consequence, lateral neighbours are deemed to expose the polysemy of the focal image. Hence, when they are presented, the user may then follow one of them by making it the focal image and explore its lateral neighbours in turn. The user interaction is immediate, since the underlying network was computed offline.

We provide the user with entry points into the database by computing a representative set of images from the collection. We cluster high-connectivity nodes and their neighbours up to a certain depth using the Markov chain clustering algorithm (van Dongen, 2000), which has robust convergence properties and allows one to specify the granularity of the clustering. The clustering result can be seen as a image database summary that shows highly-connected nodes with far-reaching connections. The right panel of Figure 4.11(a) is such a summary for our TRECVid 2003 database. The user may select any of these images as an entry point into the network. Clicking on an image moves it into the centre around which the lateral neighbours are displayed, see the nearest-neighbour panel on the left side of Figure 4.11(a). If the size of the lateral-neighbour set is above a certain threshold, the actual number of images displayed is reduced to the most salient ones.

If a user wanted to find "video shots from behind the pitcher in a baseball game as he throws a ball that the batter swings at"[4], then they might explore the database in Figure 4.11 by clicking on the falcon image. The hope is that the colour of a baseball field is not far off from the green colour of that image. The resulting lateral neighbours, displayed in the left panel of Figure 4.11(a), do not contain the desired scene. However, there is an image of a sports field. Making that the focal image, as seen in the left part of Figure 4.11(b), reveals it has the desired scene as a lateral neighbour. Clicking that will unearth a lot more images from baseball fields, see the right side of Figure 4.11(b). The network structure, a bit of lateral thinking and three mouse clicks have brought the desired result.

In the same way, and again with only three clicks, one could have started from the football image in the database overview to find "video shots from behind the pitcher in a baseball game as he throws a ball that the batter swings at". Heesch (2005) has shown that this is no coincidence; lateral-neighbour networks computed in this way have the so-called *small world property* (Watts and Strogatz, 1998) with only 3–4 degrees of separation even for the large TRECVid 2003 database that contains keyframes from 32,000 video shots. Lateral browsing has proven eminently successful for similar queries (Heesch et al, 2003).

4.5   GEO-TEMPORAL ASPECTS OF MEDIA

4.5.1   IMPORTANCE OF GEOGRAPHY AS CONTEXT

Geography is an important query element. Sanderson and Kohler (2004) identified that almost 20% of all queries in a 2001 Excite query log contained geographic elements. There is a fantastic cartoon by Saul Steinberg from the cover of the 29 March 1976 edition of the *New Yorker* that superbly expresses the prime role of location as contexts. In this sketch, called "View of the world from 9th Avenue", you see a map with details of the 9th and 10th Avenue; then East Manhattan and the Hudson river; behind that Jersey followed by the rest of the US, which takes up less space than the area between 9th and 10th Avenue; then the Pacific Ocean as big as the Hudson River with a few indiscernible stretches of tiny land labelled as China, Japan and Russia.

We may think Steinbergs cartoon in Figure 4.13 is funny, because it alludes to what some describe as the self-centric nature of New Yorkers. Wait a minute and read on: there is something else to it. When one of my former PhD students, Simon Overell, and I wanted to disambiguate placenames in free text, we decided to build a model of how placenames occur in text (Overell and Rüger, 2008).

---

[4]Topic 102 of TRECVid 2003

Figure 4.13: *View of the world from 9th Avenue*, drawing by Saul Steinberg, *The New Yorker 29* March 1976, © 2010 The Saul Steinberg Foundation/Artists Rights Society (ARS), New York, and © Condé Nast Publications

One of the best resources to study this is wikipedia, an on-line collaborative encyclopedia, where everyone can contribute articles about everything. When authors mention locations, they usually link to an article about that location. This serves to disambiguate the location. Overell (2009) identified a way to find out which articles are about locations and also which specific latitude and longitude this would be. By looking at the 2 million articles with 100 million internal links in the English language wikipedia, we obtained a large corpus of how placenames are used in the encyclopedia. The methods are language independent, and we can do the same analysis for any of the 252 languages for which wikipediae exist.

As a side effect of this pre-requisite for further research, we could visualise which locations are talked about how much in which language. It turns out that what people write about in wikipedia is strongly language dependent! Figure 4.14 shows a heat map of locations that are talked about in English.

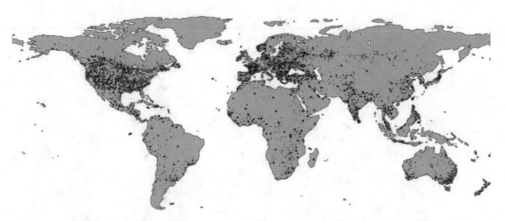

Figure 4.14: Heat map of locations referred to in the English-language wikipedia

Overell also created a video for extracted events from the year 1 CE to 2000 CE. Click at Figure 4.15 or directly at http://mmis. doc.ic.ac.uk/inaugural/events-en-sp-world.mpg to see for yourself how they compare in the English-language and Spanish-language wikipedia: watch out for the discovery of America and how the Spanish and the English maps compare at this time. I find this absolutely fascinating: it is almost as if there were two completely different worlds. Our hypothesis is that we all, not only the New Yorkers, behave, think and act like Saul Steinberg's cartoon suggests: very local, indeed!

We have created maps like these for English, Chinese, German, French, Spanish and Portuguese, which we visualised as cartograms. These are distorted world maps, see Figure 4.16: the higher the density of references to locations in a particular country (in comparison to what you would expect given the population of that country), the bigger the exaggeration of the area of that country. Yellow is an indicator for under-representative, orange for about right and red for an over-representative number of references. The Spanish and Portuguese cartograms are my favourites.

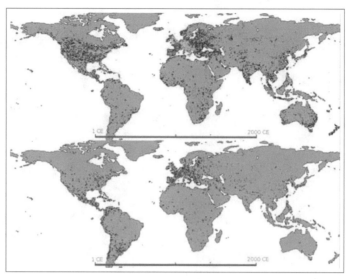

Figure 4.15: Events from 1 CE to 2000 CE of the English (top) vs the Spanish (bottom) wikipedia (click frame for video)

The "view of the world according to the Chinese wikipedia" in Figure 4.16 has the most even distribution, presumably because access to wikipedia is blocked from time to time in China and has been systematically blocked for more than a year. Hence, it is a high proportion of expatriates everywhere in the world, who contribute to wikipedia making it appear to be the most unbiased. To make it absolutely clear, this analysis is about languages, not countries! Remember, too, that most languages are spoken in more than one country and that the majority of children in the world grow up with at least two languages.

These maps convince me that we are all "little Steinbergs" be it with respect to location, our field of study, our expertise or otherwise. Hence, geography is one of the most important context factors for any kind of search engine and information provider.

4.5.2 GEO-TEMPORAL BROWSING AND ACCESS

Geo-temporal browsing takes the idea of timelines and automatically generated maps, eg as offered in the Perseus Digital Library[5], a step further. It integrates the idea of browsing in time and space with a selection of events through a text search box. In this way, a large newspaper or TV news collection can be made available through browsing based on what happened where and when as opposed to by keyword only.

The interface in Figure 4.17 is a design study in our group that allows navigation within a large news event dataset along three dimensions: time, location and text subsets. The search term presents a text filter. The temporal distribution can be seen in lower part. The overview window establishes

[5]http://www.perseus.tufts.edu

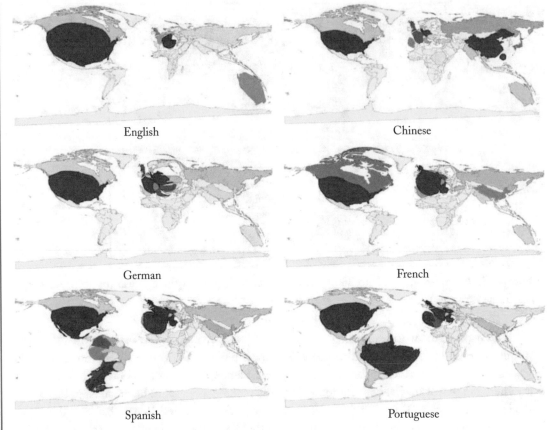

Figure 4.16: Cartograms (distorted world maps)

a frame of reference for the user's region of interest. In principle, this interface could implement new zooming techniques, eg speed-dependent automatic zooming (Cockburn and Savage, 2003), and link to a server holding a large quantity of maps such as National Geographic's MapMachine[6] with street-level maps and aerial photos.

4.6   EXERCISES

4.6.1   INTERFACE DESIGN AND FUNCTIONALITY

The NewsRoom interface in Figure 4.18 — developed on top of the ANSES technology of Section 4.1 — aims at returning the gist of the result set to the user via Information Landmarks. It lists a set of topics that were found in the search result set with the tag cloud paradigm emphasising more salient topics. At the same time, users are allowed to exclude search topics by unchecking the

[6]http://plasma.nationalgeographic.com/mapmachine as of May 2005

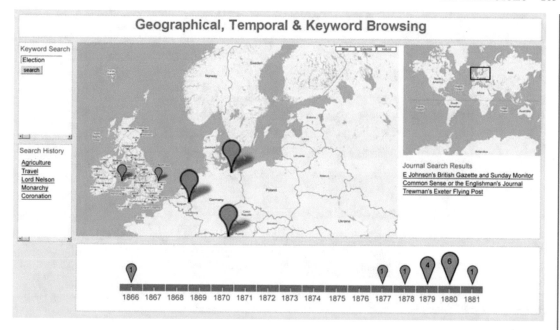

Figure 4.17: Geo-temporal browsing in action

adjacent box. News stories are put into stable categories in an attempt to help the user to browse news in a faceted way. Mousing over a story will bring up thumbnails of related videos.

Contrast the two interfaces ANSES (Figure 4.1) and NewsRoom (Figure 4.18) in terms of workflow, presented information and clarity.

4.6.2   SHOT BOUNDARY DETECTION FOR GRADUAL TRANSITIONS

Compute and plot the distance functions $d_2(t)$, $d_4(t)$, $d_8(t)$ and $d_{16}(t)$ from Equation 4.1 for a sequence of frames as depicted in Figure 4.19. You can assume the "feature values" f(t) for the frames to be $\ldots, 9, 9, 8, 7, 6, 5, 4, 3, 2, 1, 0, 0, 0, \ldots$, and the frame-distance is assumed to be $d^f(t, s) = |f(t) - f(s)|$.

Do these functions $d_n(t)$ exhibit co-inciding peaks as predicted for gradual transitions?

4.6.3   RELEVANCE FEEDBACK: OPTIMAL WEIGHT COMPUTATION

The relevance feedback model in Figure 4.9 displays the returned images on a spiral such that their distances to the centre are commensurate with the distances $D_w(m_i, q)$ of the returned images m_i to the query q. By moving one or more of the returned images either closer to the centre or farther away, the user effectively provides some real-valued feedback $D^u(m_i, q)$ as alternative to $D_w(m_i, q)$.

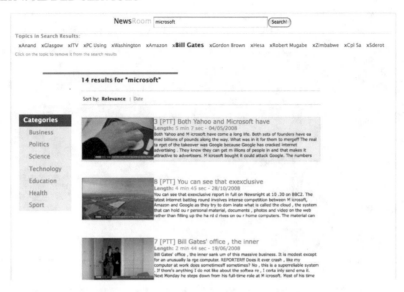

Figure 4.18: NewsRoom interface

Figure 4.19: Gradual transition of film frames

This gives rise to the squared sum of errors

$$E(w) = \sum_i (D^u(m_i, q) - D_w(m_i, q))^2.$$

Using Equation 3.11 provide an analytic solution for the optimal weight vector w such that $E(w)$ becomes minimal with respect to w.

4.6.4   RELEVANCE FEEDBACK: LAGRANGIAN MULTIPLIER

Solve the previous exercise under the constraint of convex weights.

4.6.5   GEOGRAPHIC ATTRIBUTES

You would like to attach geographic features to multimedia objects and decide to consult the CIA world factbook https://www.cia.gov/library/publications/the-world-factbook to add information about the history, people, government, economy, geography, communications, transportation, military, and transnational issues beyond the trivial latitude and longitude coordinates. Explain which features you select, how you standardise them, and which distance measures you suggest for these.

4.6.6   VIEW OF THE WORLD — RETRIEVAL AND CONTEXT

Our gifted lab artist Jon Linney created an analogous version of Steinberg's cartoon (Figure 4.13) for London's Piccadilly Circus, see Figure 4.20. Make a similar sketch for were you live. Incorporate all places that are important to you. Think about other context variables, for example, related to your music taste or your daily work. In your mind, does IR stand for infrared, information retrieval or International Rectifier (a company producing products for power management)? Which variables describe context and how could they be incorporated into multimedia retrieval?

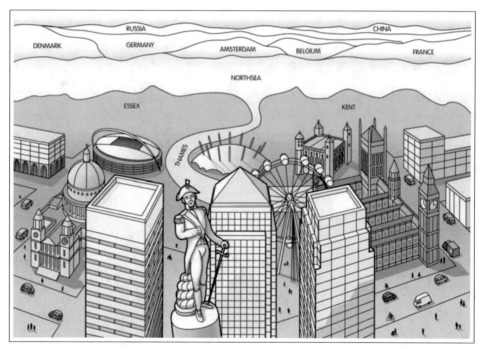

Figure 4.20: View of the world from Piccadilly Circus

CHAPTER 5

Multimedia Information Retrieval Research

In this chapter, we look at a number of current, cutting-edge research projects in the wider area of multimedia information retrieval and at the visions that drive the state of the art. It is organised by the following key research themes:

- *Multimedia representation and management* as the basis of any retrieval technology
- *Digital libraries* to utilise existing metadata and to integrate multimedia in conventional digital libraries other than via traditional metadata library cards
- *Metadata and automated annotation* to bridge the semantic gap in multimedia information retrieval
- *User needs and evaluation* to put the user at the centre of the tasks requiring multimedia information retrieval
- *Multimedia search and mining systems* how to find and access multimedia for a given resource discovery mission
- *Browsing and presentation of multimedia data* for publishing and consuming multimedia information

5.1 MULTIMEDIA REPRESENTATION AND MANAGEMENT

In this section, I make a distinction between data-driven multimedia representation and knowledge-based methods. For the former, the media itself are the focus of attention, while the latter look more at applications that process knowledge in one form or another.

Data-driven methods. Current research in multimedia data management spans a variety of problems including handling of duplicates and document overlaps for multimedia (see also the fingerprinting techniques of Section 2.5) and meta-search engines (Wu et al, 2004b); optimising the indexing of high-dimensional feature spaces (see Subsection 3.5), which are very typical for content-based multimedia retrieval; combining and selecting low-level visual features for retrieval (Howarth and Rüger, 2005b; Hilaire and Jose, 2007); indexing photograph collections in the form of simple relations between concepts as opposed to keyword indexing (Martinet et al, 2003); developing visual attention algorithms for region of interest coding that produce an "interest ordered" progressive bit-stream in JPEG2000 so that the regions highlighted by the algorithm are presented first in bit-stream (Bradley and Stentiford, 2003); generating motion vectors for scalable video coding (Mrak et al, 2004); preserving privacy for video-based applications (Cavallaro, 2004); supporting retrieval on small devices through hierarchical-query biased summaries (Sweeney and Crestani, 2004); representing and retrieving images from a collection of scientific articles using the text encapsulated in their XML structure (Kong and Lalmas, 2007); analysing and treating semantic relations between terms (Cai and van Rijsbergen, 2005); and creating eminently browsable graphical networks between multimedia objects to represent semantic and content-based facets of their respective similarity (Heesch and Rüger, 2005).

Calic et al (2005) carried out a critical survey of the methods for video representation targeting semantic analysis and outlining the importance of multimodal approaches for multimedia information retrieval.

There have been attempts to add self-management to multimedia servers, for example, in autonomic systems (Huebscher and McCann, 2008); for news-like sites their system is able to measure user context and system trends to decide how best to serve the multimedia artefact to the user.

This wide cross-section of research activity is also mirrored and supported by formal projects such as the UK-funded GATE project, see Subsection 5.1.1, a framework architecture for text engineering; AXMEDIS (5.1.2) that aims to speed up and optimise content production and distribution for production-on-demand; NM2 (5.1.3) that develops new interactive media forms; 3DTV (5.1.4), a research network to further 3d television; and VISNET II (5.1.5), a EU network of excellence in the area of audiovisual media technologies.

All these projects are engaged to further the state of the art in one or more of the dimensions of standards, automation, intelligent handling of data and supporting creativity.

Knowledge-based methods. Most of the work in knowledge-based multimedia management is rather recent, and some noticeable projects have made progress in this area: X-Media studied knowledge that is distributed in different media (images, documents and data) in complex distributed environments, see Subsection 5.1.6); MediaCampaign automated the detection and tracking of advertisement campaigns on television, internet and in the press, for example, via logo tracking (5.1.7); SALERO looked at reusing media objects across media to improve production of games, movies and broadcast (5.1.8); LUISA developed content management system for learning objects using a semantic web services architecture (5.1.9); SEMEDIA developed a collection of audiovisual tools such as video browsing tools, tag exploration tools for Flickr, video tagging games that were integrated into a post-production data repository and a broadcast data archive (5.1.10).

Knowledge-based multimedia representation involves a wide spectrum of approaches. Some, eg, Chakravarthy et al (2006), develop strategies and interfaces for cross-media knowledge creation and sharing that make references between text and images in multimedia documents explicit with a view to increasing the value of the document itself. In a similar spirit Liu et al (2007) and Magalhães and Rüger (2007) deploy automated classification and machine learning of concepts to add knowledge to image descriptions. Gardoni et al (2005) developed a groupware tool that supports *asynchronous* work on industrial drawings and sketches. The significance of this work is the possible re-use of sketches after they have been created. Later (ie, asynchronous) re-use is normally very difficult as the meaning of symbols and elements in sketches depends on the (synchronous) agreement amongst the users of the sketch at creation time.

On the other end of this spectrum, Potter et al (2007) developed and analysed an integrated system that applies recent ideas and technologies from the fields of Artificial Intelligence and Semantic Web research to support sense- and decision-making at the tactical response level. They demonstrate their approach with reference to a hypothetical large-scale emergency scenario.

5.1.1   GATE

GATE[1] (General Architecture for Text Engineering) is a programming environment, which enables users to develop and deploy language engineering components and resources in a robust fashion (Cunningham et al, 2002). The GATE architecture supports a number of applications for language processing tasks such as information extraction. The framework can be used to develop applications and resources in multiple languages, based on its Unicode support throughout. GATE is open source Java software under the GNU library licence, and it is a robust and scalable infrastructure, which allows users to build and customise language processing components, while everyday tasks like data storage, format analysis and data visualisation are handled by GATE. The system is bundled with components for language analysis, and is in use for information extraction, information retrieval, natural language generation, summarisation, dialogue, semantic web and digital libraries applications. GATE-based systems have taken part in the all the major quantitative evaluation programmes for natural language processing since 1995. Nowadays, GATE is a popular choice for both the handling and analysis of text in multimedia projects and applications.

5.1.2   AXMEDIS

AXMEDIS[2] (Automating Production of Cross Media Content for Multi-channel Distribution) was an EU-funded integrated project (2004–2008), led by Università di Firenze, Italy. It built methods and tools to speed up and optimise content production and distribution for production-on-demand situations. The project specifically looked at automation for integrating content management systems with distribution systems. The content model and manipulation exploits and expands MPEG-4, MPEG-7 and MPEG-21 and other real and de-facto standards. AXMEDIS objects are specific MPEG-21 objects. The project created demonstrators, validated through activities with end-users in the area of content production, for both business-to-business distribution and for i-TV-PC, PCs, mobiles and PDAs.

During its lifetime, the project organised an annual conference on Automated Production of Cross Media Content for Multi-Channel Distribution. AXMEDIA's web site continues to distribute tools to manipulate AXMEDIA objects such as editors, media players, content processing tools, legal peer-to-peer sharing tools based on the BitTorrent protocol, digital rights management tools, and portals that demonstrate AXMEDIS content and distribution.

[1] http://gate.ac.uk
[2] http://www.axmedis.org

5.1.3   NM2

NM2[3] (New Media for the New Millennium) was an EU-funded integrated project (2004–2007), led by BT Group, UK, in which creative and technology experts participated to develop new media forms that take advantage of the unique characteristics of broadband networks. The project was about creating a new media genre using all of the facilities of interactive terminals, for example, shows where viewers are able to interact directly with the medium and influence what they see and hear according to their personal tastes and wishes.

Sussner et al (2006) discuss a multimedia 3d interface for the NM2 interactive movie *Gormenghast Explore* that enables viewers to reconfigure personalised video sequences in real-time. This production is a re-edit of 4 hours of footage of the BBC Millennium series *Gormenghast* that was televised in January 2001. Altogether, four NM2 pilot productions (*Gods in the Sky Choice*, *Cambridge City Symphony*, *Gormenghast Explore*, and *RuneCast*) were demonstrated at the 27th Cambridge International Film Festival in 2007.

5.1.4   3DTV

3DTV[4] (Integrated Three-Dimensional Television — Capture, Transmission, and Display) was an EU-funded network of excellence (2004–2008), with a consortium of 20 organisations led by the Bilkent University, Turkey. 3DTV was about the development towards a more realistic television experience by capturing three-dimensional real-life scenes and re-creating a visual representation at a remote site. The primary goal of this network was to deal with all aspects of 3d television, such as the capture and representation of 3d scene information, the definition of digital 3d TV signals, their storage and transmission, and finally, the display of the reproduced 3d scene, in an integrated manner. As part of this project Onural et al (2006) gave an overview of 3d TV technologies.

5.1.5   VISNET II

VISNET II[5] (Networked audiovisual media technologies) was an EU-funded network of excellence (2006–2009) that was comprised of 12 European organisations in the field of networked audiovisual media technologies. The project was coordinated by the Centre for Communication Systems Research (CCSR), a part of an academic school at the University of Surrey. VISNET II consortium members conducted integration, research and dissemination activities in three main topics: video coding, audiovisual media processing and multimedia security. *Video coding* techniques enable rich visual services with scalable formats, coding efficiency, and error resilience and scalability with emphasis on quality optimisation even under adverse networking conditions. *Audiovisual content analysis* enhances the personalised and seamless access to audio visual content, covering topics such as metadata extraction techniques, automated annotation, human body detection and tracking, face recognition as well as music, audio and speech analysis. *Distributed and secure access platforms* utilise

---

[3]http://www.ist-nm2.org
[4]http://www.3dtv-research.org
[5]http://www.visnet-noe.org

middleware layers and provide the architectural support for interoperability and context-aware, adaptable services, and cross-network delivery of audio visual content via low power terminals and low-complexity techniques.

5.1.6   X-MEDIA

X-Media[6] (Large Scale Knowledge Management across Media) was an EU-funded integrated project (2006–2009) led by the University of Sheffield. It studied knowledge management in complex distributed environments, researched, developed and implemented large-scale methodologies and techniques for knowledge management with a view to supporting sharing and reuse of knowledge that was distributed in different media (images, documents and data) and repositories (data bases, knowledge bases, document repositories, etc). X-Media put a focus on seamless integration with current work practices emphasising usability and ease of customisation for new applications. Its goal was to improve access to, sharing of and use of information by humans as well as by and between machines. The work was driven by real world requirements taken from case studies at Rolls Royce (jet engines) and Fiat (cars). Rolls Royce tested life cycle monitoring, and Fiat carried out competitor analysis. The multimedia in this project are data from sensors and cameras that need to be interpreted. Its textual documents complement, describe, and help interpreting the multimedia data, while ontologies describe the domain and the application. Petrelli et al (2009) demonstrated in a case study within X-Media how a visualization of semantic data according to some easy dimensions such as space and time provides effective sense-making of data. They looked holistically at the interaction between users and semantic data, and proposed multiple visualization strategies and dynamic filters to support the exploration of semantic-rich data.

5.1.7   MEDIACAMPAIGN

MediaCampaign[7] (Discovering, inter-relating and navigating cross-media campaign knowledge) was a EU-funded specific targeted research project (2006–2008) coordinated by Joanneum Research, Austria. The project's main goal was to automatically detect and track media campaigns on television, internet and in the press. For the pilot system developed within the project, the focus was on advertisement campaigns, for example, the tracking of logos and their exposure at car races. This is currently a manual process. Scientifically the project was focused on the creation of a knowledge model for the semantic description of media campaigns; the automated identification and tracking of new media campaigns in different media; and modelling of domain-specific ontologies, which relate media campaigns over different media and countries.

---

[6]http://www.x-media-project.org
[7]http://www.media-campaign.eu

5.1.8   SALERO

SALERO[8] (Semantic AudiovisuaL Entertainment Reusable Objects) was an EU-funded integrated project (2006–2009). It aimed at making cross-media production for games, movies and broadcast faster, better and cheaper by combining computer graphics, language technology, semantic web technologies as well as content based search and retrieval. SALERO defined and developed content for media productions, consisting of multimedia objects with context-aware behaviours for self-adaptive use and delivery across different platforms. This content should enable the creation and re-use of complex media by artists who do not need to know the technical aspects of these tools (Thallinger et al, 2009).

5.1.9   LUISA

LUISA[9] (Learning Content Management System Using Innovative Semantic Web Services Architecture) was an EU-funded specific targeted research project (2006–2008), coordinated by Atos Origin, Spain. LUISA developed a reference semantic architecture for search, interchange and delivery of learning objects in a service-oriented context. More specifically, the project developed a semantic web service-based architecture for discovery, selection, negotiation, composition and semantic annotation of learning resources. Dietze et al (2007) show how to deploy this and mappings between different learning metadata standards as well as ontological concepts for e-learning. They later (2009) go one step further and propose Situation-driven Learning Processes (SDLP), which describe learning processes semantically from two perspectives: the user perspective that considers them as a course of learning goals, whereas the system perspective utilizes Semantic Web Services (SWS) technology to semantically describe necessary resources for each learning goal within a specific learning situation.

5.1.10   SEMEDIA

SEMEDIA[10] (Search Environments for Media) was a specific targeted research project of the EU, led by Fundacio Barcelona Media Universitat Pompeu Fabra (2007–2009). It developed a collection of audiovisual search and navigation tools that are generic enough to be applicable to the different fields of broadcasting production, cinema post-production and social web. Two example techniques from this project include diversifying image search with user generated content (van Zwol et al, 2008) and Flickr tag recommendation based on collective knowledge (Sigurbjörnsson and van Zwol, 2008).

5.2   DIGITAL LIBRARIES

Digital libraries raise the amount, availability, accessibility, assortment and authority of information. Museums, film and music archives are increasingly turning towards digital versions of their artifacts,

---

[8]http://www.salero.info
[9]http://www.luisa-project.eu
[10]http://www.semedia.org

partly for keeping digital records, partly for preservation and partly for increasing access. Hence, multimedia digital libraries become increasingly more important.

Distinctive institutions to further the development, implementation and uptake of (multimedia) digital libraries are the US National Science Foundation that created a US online library for education and research in Science, Technology, Engineering and Mathematics[11]; the British Library[12] with its British Library Research and Innovation Centre[13]; and UKOLN[14], a centre of excellence in digital information management, providing advice and services to the library, information and cultural heritage communities.

Digital libraries mainly provide three things: preservation of digital objects, an infrastructure to ingress material, and access to content.

Preservation. PrestoSpace[15] (Preservation towards storage and access) was an EU-funded project (2004–2008) that contributed to technical solutions and integrated systems for digital preservation of all types of audiovisual collections in the domain of restoration, storage and archive management, content description, delivery and access. Some further examples for work on digital preservation include the US National Digital Information Infrastructure and Preservation Programme[16], the UK Digital Curation Centre[17], as well as other European projects such as Digital Preservation Europe[18], PLANETS[19] and CASPAR[20].

Infrastructure. This decides how easy it is to adapt existing digital library software to build digital collections, ingress multimedia objects and distribute the collections. One of the most versatile and widely used platforms for this is the open-source Greenstone digital library software described in Subsection 5.2.1.

Access. The Open Archives Initiative[21] (OAI) aims to provide low-barrier interoperability for digital libraries and archives. The main point is to allow service providers to harvest metadata, so they can provide value-added services, which can be as simple as combining different repositories. Lagoze and Van de Sompel, both serve as the OAI executive, review the history of the OAI and describe how the protocol for metadata harvesting came about (2003).

The most salient and earliest of the multimedia digital library research projects for access is Informedia (see Subsection 5.2.2) at Carnegie Mellon University. Other notable large projects are SCULPTEUR that specialised in 3d models of museum objects (5.2.3); CHLT that created tools for studying and understanding ancient languages (5.2.4); DELOS, a network of excellence concerned with developing a digital library Reference Model (see 5.2.5); BRICKS, which was a

[11]http://nsdl.org
[12]http://www.bl.uk
[13]http://www.ukoln.ac.uk/services/papers/bl
[14]http://www.ukoln.ac.uk
[15]http://prestospace.org
[16]http://www.digitalpreservation.gov
[17]http://www.dcc.ac.uk
[18]http://www.digitalpreservationeurope.eu
[19]http://www.planets-project.eu
[20]http://www.casparpreserves.eu
[21]http://www.openarchives.org

concerted effort to create a shared digital library of distributed resources from museums and archives (5.2.6). StoryBank, which was a UK-funded digital library project that aimed to share stories across digital divides (5.2.7).

eChase[22] (Electronic Cultural Heritage made Accessible for Sustainable Exploitations) was a European project with a different mission altogether, namely to investigate sustainable business models to commercialise and exploit content in museums and archives (Sinclair et al, 2005).

A series of projects on use and usability of digital libraries have been based at University College London. The most recent of these projects are User-Centred Interactive Search (UCIS, 2004–2008) and Making Sense of Information (MaSI, 2006–2009). The UCIS project has been investigating the practices and needs of Humanities scholars, including understanding the relationships between physical and digital media (Rimmer et al, 2008) and how people find and work with information in different formats. The MaSI project has studied how people make sense of information, integrating information from multiple sources and in multiple formats. It has investigated novel visualization techniques for representing and working with information. Earlier work, eg by Blandford et al (2004), investigated analytical usability evaluations for digital libraries, ie, assessing these by usability professionals using established theories and methods. In another study, Blandford and Stelmaszewska (2002) evaluated four web-accessible music libraries, focusing particularly on features that are specific to music libraries, such as music retrieval mechanisms and modalities. A framework for planning evaluation studies for such systems has been presented by Blandford et al (2008).

5.2.1   GREENSTONE

The principal research output of the Digital Libraries Research group[23] at the University of Waikato, NZ, is called Greenstone[24], which is an open source, multilingual digital library toolkit. It enables you to create collections of digital content straight away, which are then accessed and searched in a web browser. Greenstone can be configured to work either over the Internet, an intranet, or stand-alone from DVDs (or similar). It runs on all major platforms, and it is mobile and screen-aware for hand-held devices such as the iPod.

Various UN agencies and other Non-Government Organisations use Greenstone to provide self-contained fully searchable CD-ROMS on humanitarian aid to developing countries. Regional workshops and tutorials[25], partly run by UNESCO, take place all over the world as far-flung away as Micronesia. Greenstone is downloaded 200 times/day, 70,000/year, and it has user bases in every continent. Through UNESCO sponsorship the software is fully documented in English, French, Spanish, and Russian. In addition, its web interface has been translated into 55 languages by enthusiastic volunteers. The project's positive social impact has been acknowledged through the

---

[22] http://www.echase.org
[23] http://nzdl.sadl.uleth.ca/cgi-bin/library
[24] http://www.greenstone.org
[25] http://www.greenstone.org/map

the biennial Namur award[26], which recognizes recipients for raising awareness internationally of the social implications of information and communication technologies.

Countless digital libraries have been built with Greenstone since its public release on Source-Forge in 2000: from historic Māori newspapers to a collection of WHO documents for disasters; from first aid in pictures to curated first editions of works by Chopin; from scientific institutional repositories to personal collections of photos and other document formats.

Witten and Bainbridge's textbook (2002) on how to build a digital library — the two authors lead the Greenstone project — has just been published in a second edition (Witten et al, 2010).

5.2.2   INFORMEDIA

Informedia[27] is an umbrella for a number of digital video library research projects, most of which deal with video understanding in the widest sense, including search, retrieval, visualisation and summarisation for videos, both digitally born or digitised. The first of these projects, now called Informedia I[28] (1994-1999), built base technologies to process digital videos: it performed automated speech recognition and combined speech, image and natural language understanding to automatically transcribe, segment and index linear video for search and image retrieval.

The Informedia suite of projects has brought about much original research: Hauptmann (2005) gave an overview of 10 years of Informedia research, while Hauptmann et al (2007) speculate on how many semantic concepts would be needed to bridge the semantic gap in broadcast news retrieval, and how they should be selected and used. They examined extreme video retrieval that relates to video retrieval as extreme programming related to programming (Hauptmann et al, 2006), while Lin and Hauptmann (2008) attempt to determine news broadcasters' ideological perspective. The Informedia team have applied their technologies in applications spanning from oral history digital libraries Christel et al (2006) to pervasive audiovisual analysis in nursing care homes in their CareMedia project (Hauptmann et al, 2004).

5.2.3   SCULPTEUR

SCULPTEUR[29] (Semantic and content-based multimedia exploitation for European benefit) was a EU-funded project (2002–2006) that aimed to help create, manage and present cultural archives of 3d models and associated multimedia objects (Addis et al, 2003, 2005). SCULPTEUR creates 3d object representations and stores them in an object relational database together with multimedia objects, which enrich the information associated with the cultural objects. 3d object retrieval algorithms have been developed along with a semantic layer of ontologies. Multimedia objects and objects derived from them are associated with concepts in this semantic layer. In SCULPTEUR, browsing, retrieval and navigation are enabled through the use of integrated content and concept-based queries. Users are allowed to access the information from the museum partners collaborating

---

[26]http://www.info.fundp.ac.be/~jbl/IFIP/award.html
[27]http://www.informedia.cs.cmu.edu
[28]http://www.informedia.cs.cmu.edu/dli1/index.html
[29]http://www.SCULPTEURweb.org

in the project structured through a common ontology. All these have been integrated into an existing image digital library system to create a robust, scalable and distributed multimedia digital library infrastructure.

5.2.4   CHLT

CHLT[30] (Cultural Heritage Language Technologies) (Carey et al, 2003; Rydberg-Cox, 2005; Rydberg-Cox et al, 2004) was a collaborative joint US-EU project (2002–2005) to create computational tools for the study of Ancient Greek, Early Modern Latin and Old Norse texts in a network of affiliated digital libraries.

The CHLT project has provided access to rare and fragile source materials by creating corpora of Early-Modern Latin and Old Icelandic texts; transcriptions, images and hand-coded texts of over 60,000 words of Newton manuscripts in fully searchable form; and a digital library environment that allows for high resolution images of pages from rare and fragile printed books and manuscripts to be presented alongside these automatically generated hypertexts so that users can read the texts and see the pages on which they originally appeared.

The project helped readers understand texts written in difficult languages by creating parsers for Old Norse and Early-Modern Latin that automatically identify the grammatical identity of a word; by integrating these parsers into a digital library reading environment that automatically generates hypertexts where a user can click on a word, see its identity and look it up in a dictionary; and by building a multi-lingual information retrieval tool that allows users to enter queries in English and search texts written in Greek and Latin.

CHLT enabled scholars to conduct new types of scholarship by developing an innovative visualization tool that clusters these search results in conceptual categories; using computational techniques to build a word-profile tool that integrates statistical data, information from different reference works and citations of passages into a single interface; and by creating tools that allow for the computational study of style.

5.2.5   DELOS

DELOS[31] was a network of excellence on digital libraries, funded by the EU between 2004–2007. The main objective of DELOS was to coordinate a joint programme of activities of 55 European teams working in digital library related areas. The network developed a Digital Library Reference Model, which has the needs of next-generation systems in mind, and implemented a globally integrated prototype of a Digital Library Management System, called DelosDLMS, which serves as a partial implementation of the reference model.

---

[30]http://www.chlt.org
[31]http://www.delos.info

5.2.6   BRICKS

BRICKS[32] (Building Resources for Integrated Cultural Knowledge Services) was an integrated project funded by the EU during 2004–2007, which was coordinated by Engineering Ingegneria Informatica SpA, an Italian IT integrator. BRICKS aimed at integrating the existing digital resources into a common and shared digital library covering Digital Museums and Digital Archives. It researched and implemented open-source software solutions for sharing and exploiting digital cultural resources. The project established a community of cultural heritage institutions, research organisations, technological providers and other players in the field of digital libraries services.

5.2.7   STORYBANK

StoryBank[33] was a UK-funded project, which started in 2006. It has allowed village communities in the developing world to create and share audiovisual information easily. This information could range from health or agricultural advice to reporting personal local news. Camera phones and digital library software were used to create and share short audiovisual stories meaning any spoken report, illustrated with still or moving images. StoryBank's main rationale was to give a stronger voice and role to people who cannot read, write or use text on the internet. By setting up a repository and connecting that to the internet, StoryBank has allowed people to share locally and across the digital divide. Jones et al (2008) provided a first prototype of the system.

5.3   METADATA AND AUTOMATED ANNOTATION

Two recent EU-funded networks of excellence have been concerned with bridging the semantic gap: MUSCLE[34] (Multimedia Understanding through Semantics, Computation and Learning 2004–2008) and K-Space[35] (Knowledge Space of Semantic Inference for automated annotation and retrieval of Multimedia Content 2006–2008). Another EU integrated project, aceMedia (see 5.3.1) has the specific aim of generating automated annotations from content to make it easier to find and re-use content.

Some of the fundamental tasks for generating metadata automatically are rooted in machine learning tasks of classification and pattern analysis. One notable current EU-funded network of excellence in this area is PASCAL2 (Pattern Analysis, Statistical Modelling and Computational Learning), which builds on the PASCAL[36] network of excellence that pioneers principled methods of pattern analysis, statistical modelling, and computational learning (Rousu et al, 2006; Lodhi et al, 2002a; Shawe-Taylor and Cristianini, 2002). Two other EU projects that deploy machine learning for object recognition and classification are LAVA, see Subsection 5.3.2, and KerMIT, see Subsec-

---

[32]http://www.brickscommunity.org
[33]http://cs.swan.ac.uk/storybank
[34]http://www.muscle-noe.org
[35]http://kspace.qmul.net
[36]http://www.pascal-network.org

tion 5.3.3. The books by Cristianini and Shawe-Taylor (2000) and Shawe-Taylor and Cristianini (2004) provide a summary of a much of the PASCAL, KerMIT and LAVA orientations.

POLYMNIA (5.3.4) is a recently finished EU project that allows museum visits to be shared with friends and family via live video stream and recorded on a DVD.

The Humanities Advanced Technology and Information Institute (HATII), University of Glasgow, has been examining methods of achieving automated semantic metadata extraction from digital documents as a crucial step in realising automated ingest, selection and management of digital material. As a step in this direction, Kim and Ross have been looking at automated genre classification as an essential area of study that will bind efforts in genre-specific automated metadata and provide structural classification of unstructured text for mining, both from a digital library perspective (2007) and from a language processing perspective (2008).

The recent UK-funded project ANAWIKI[37] (Creating anaphorically annotated resources through semantic wikis, 2007–2009) attempts to create metadata on a large scale using the community. These metadata complement a linguistic corpus with vital information on the correct reference of words such as he, she, it, which etc. Their meaning in sentences such as *The monkey took the banana into the tree-house and ate it* are eminently clear to humans, but state-of-the-art automated natural-language processing still struggles with the so-called problem of anaphora resolution: does *it* refer to the tree-house or the banana? In some sense, anaphora resolution is one of the semantic gaps in natural-language processing, and building large-scale annotated corpora are undoubtedly a vital contribution to the research field.

The ANAWIKI project at the University of Essex adopts the idea of "games for a purpose" of von Ahn and Dabbish (2004) discussed in 2.4 and tries to turn the chore of annotation into an enjoyable experience by amateurs. The project has developed tools to allow and encourage large numbers of volunteers over the Web to collaborate in the creation of semantically annotated corpora.

5.3.1   ACEMEDIA

aceMedia[38] (Integrating knowledge, semantics and content for user-centered intelligent media services) was an EU-funded integrated project (2004–2007) coordinated by Motorola Ltd, UK. The project aimed at integrating knowledge, semantics and content for user-centred intelligent media services. aceMedia has focussed on developing a system to extract and exploit meaning inherent to the content in order to automate annotation and to add functionality that makes it easier for all users to create, communicate, find, consume and re-use content. aceMedia targets knowledge discovery and embedded self-adaptability to enable content to be self organising, self annotating, self associating; more readily searched (faster, more relevant results) and adaptable to user requirements (self reformatting).

---

[37]http://www.anawiki.org
[38]http://www.acemedia.org

5.3.2   LAVA

LAVA[39] (Learning for Adaptable Visual Assistants, 2002–2005) created fundamental enabling technologies for cognitive vision systems and extended our understanding of the systems- and user-level aspects of their applications (Lodhi et al, 2002b; Cristianini et al, 2002; Vinokourov et al, 2002). Technologically, the objectives were the robust and efficient categorisation and interpretation of large numbers of objects, scenes and events, in real settings, and automatic online acquisition of knowledge of categories, for convenient construction of applications. Categorisation is fundamentally a generalisation problem, which was addressed using measures of distance between visual descriptors known as "kernels". The project improved generalisation performance by incorporating prior knowledge about the behaviour of descriptors within kernels and by exploiting the large amounts of unlabelled data available to vision systems.

5.3.3   KERMIT

KerMIT[40] (Kernel Methods for Image and Text) developed and tested intelligent research prototypes for document classification, filtering, ranking and clustering for a massive multi-lingual, multimedia data collection through the application of novel statistically well-founded machine learning methods (Hardoon et al, 2004; Farquhar et al, 2005; Hardoon et al, 2006). This EU project (2001–2004) was coordinated by Royal Holloway, University of London, and involved two commercial and four university partners. The kernel-based techniques were applied to text, images and general multi-media data to demonstrate how the kernel provides an interface between the data specifics and the particular algorithmic demands. Hence, the main objectives fell into three headings: development of (1) adaptive document filtering and categorisation, (2) adaptive document ranking, (3) document clustering. In order to achieve these objectives, there was technical development of specific kernels for different languages and data types, semantic refinement of kernels, kernel-based algorithm development, and its statistical analysis.

5.3.4   POLYMNIA

POLYMNIA[41] was an EU-funded specific targeted research project between 2004 and 2007, which was coordinated by the Institute of Communication and Computer Systems, Greece. POLYMNIA is an intelligent cross-media platform for the production of custom video souvenirs for visitors to leisure and cultural heritage venues. Visitors are visually tracked by cameras as they enjoy a venue. Live video stream channels are constantly available to friends and family so they can share in the visitors experience at the venue. A personalized DVD, or a less expensive eCard, is produced at the end of a visitor's stay as a souvenir, which can be purchased, allowing visitors to relive their experiences at the park well after the initial visit. POLYMNIA technology scales well to large venues, such as

---

[39] http://www.ecs.soton.ac.uk/research/projects/LAVA
[40] http://www.euro-kermit.org
[41] http://polymnia.pc.unicatt.it

theme parks or museums, and has been installed and tested in a real theme park as part of the final project evaluation.

5.4   USER NEEDS AND EVALUATION

User needs. Cooniss et al (2000, 2003) carried out two widely noted studies of the needs, characteristics, and actions of end users of visual information in the workplace (called VISOR 1 and 2). VISOR 2 created a user-oriented evaluation framework for the development of electronic image retrieval systems in the workplace during a one year project in 2000. One of the useful distinctions in their reports is the one between searching for oneself and searching as an intermediary, eg, for a journalist on the other side of the phone.

Smeulders et al (2000) identified three types of search, labelled 'target search', aiming at a specific multimedia object identified by title or other metadata; 'category search', where the user has no specific object in mind but can describe which features they would like; and 'search by association' where the user is less specific and happy to browse in order to retrieve multimedia by serendipity.

For archival collections one would expect that most requests are likely to be for target searches, which reflects the nature of curated collections and their users. One of the earliest studies that confirmed this expectation analysed some 2,700 requests to the Hulton Deutsch collection, now part of Getty Images[42] (Enser and McGregor, 1992; Enser, 1993). A number of other studies have reported a relatively high proportion of requests for specific and named features (Armitage and Enser, 1997; Chen, 2001), and, in the particular context of requests by journalists to newspaper picture archives (Ornager, 1995; Markkula and Sormunen, 2000). The user studies reported by Hollink et al (2004), Choi and Rasmussen (2002), Frost and Noakes (1998), Hastings (1995), and Keister (1994) support the general observation that the further one moves away from specialist archival collections towards less constrained environments the more pronounced becomes the emphasis on search by association and category searches for more generic multimedia. Jörgensen and Jörgensen (2005) studied the search behaviour of image professionals for advertising, marketing and graphic design, by analysing search logs from a commercial image subscription service. Here a very low proportion of the requests were for specifically named features; instead, there was a preference for thematic terms and browsing.

At the non-professional end of the spectrum for image search Goodrum and Spink (2001) analysed transaction logs of over 33,000 image requests submitted to the Excite search engine by 10,000 searchers with otherwise unknown characteristics: they found a high rate of search modification, with sexual or adult content terms dominating the hundred most frequently occurring terms. In a more general user study (Tombros et al, 2005) investigated the criteria used by online searchers when assessing the relevance of web pages for information-seeking tasks.

Adapt and VIRAMI, described in Subsections 5.4.1 and 5.4.2, are two projects concerned with user needs: the first one technology driven, the other one application driven.

---

[42]http://www.gettyimages.com

Evaluation. Since its early conception information retrieval as a subject has always placed great emphasis on system evaluation. Real user needs are simulated in a laboratory setting with three ingredients: *large test collections, information need statements* and *relevance judgements*. The test collection contains a large number of potentially interesting documents from a repository; each information need statement details the type of document that the user would like to retrieve, what the user hopes to see or hear and criteria for how the relevance of documents should be judged. The relevance judgements, also known as *ground truth*, tell us whether a particular document of the collection is relevant for a particular information need. The value of an evaluation setting like this is that the effectiveness of a particular retrieval method can be measured in a *reproducible* way. Although this approach has been criticised for its lack of realism and its narrow focus on the pure retrieval aspect of presumably much bigger real tasks, system evaluations are still the main basis on which retrieval algorithms are judged, and on the back of which research flourishes.

In this respect evaluation conferences such as INEX for structured XML retrieval (see Subsection 5.4.3), TRECVid for video retrieval (5.4.4), ImageCLEF for image retrieval (5.4.5), GeoCLEF for geographic retrieval (5.4.6) and MIREX for music retrieval (5.4.7) have a significant and lasting impact on science through reproducibility and comparisons.

5.4.1   ADAPT

The UK-funded Adapt[43] (Adaptive Search Models for Information Retrieval) project (2005–2006) at the University of Glasgow has created search models that adapt to the information needs of the searcher (Joho and Jose, 2008). These models use implicit methods to unobtrusively monitor searcher interaction, make inferences about what constitutes relevant material, create new queries and choose appropriate retrieval strategies. The search models Adapt has created are based on implicit feedback by incorporating the role of context and the development of structured presentation techniques.

5.4.2   VIRAMI

VIRAMI[44] (Visual Information Retrieval for Archival Moving Imagery) systematically analysed client information need for heritage film and video, together with a survey of subject content representation and cataloguing practice in film archives. VIRAMI also considered the role that content-based image retrieval techniques might play in simplifying some of the metadata construction. The survey revealed a marked lack of consistency in cataloguing and indexing practice and at the same time a common need to address the emphasis that clients place on retrieving footage with specifically named persons, objects, places and events, and combinations of these facets (Enser and Sandom, 2002). This finding substantiated the view expressed by all the survey participants that content-based techniques did not, at the time, offer a generally effective alternative to the textual subject description for accessing the videos.

---

[43]http://www.dcs.gla.ac.uk/~jj/projects/adapt
[44]http://www.brighton.ac.uk/cmis/research/groups/vir

5.4.3   INEX XML MULTIMEDIA TRACK

In 2002, the INEX[45] Initiative for the Evaluation of XML Retrieval started to provide a test-bed for evaluation of effective access to structured XML content. The organisation of INEX passed from the University of Duisburg to Otago University[46] in the year 2008.

Van Zwol et al (2005) set up an XML multimedia track that was repeated as part of INEX until 2007. It provided a pilot evaluation platform for structured document retrieval systems that combine multiple media types. While in 2005 the collection was made up from Lonely Planet travel guides, the 2006 evaluations used the much larger Wikipedia collection from the INEX main track (Westerveld and van Zwol, 2006). Both collections contain a range of media, including text, image speech, and video — thus modelling real life structured documents. The goal of the multimedia track was to investigate multimedia retrieval from a new perspective, using the structure of documents as the semantic and logical backbone for the retrieval of multimedia fragments.

In contrast to other evaluation fora, INEX's multimedia track was to retrieve relevant document fragments based on an information need with a structured multimedia character, ie, it focused on the use of document structure to estimate, relate, and combine the relevance of different multimedia fragments. One big challenge for a structured document retrieval system is to combine the relevance of the different media types and XML elements into a single meaningful ranking that can be presented to the user.

5.4.4   TRECVID

The TREC Video Retrieval Evaluation initiative (TRECVid[47]) is an independent evaluation forum devoted to research in automatic segmentation, indexing, and content-based retrieval of digital video. It started out in 2001 as a video track of the TREC[48] conference series and became an independent 2-day workshop of is own in 2003. TRECVid is sponsored by the NIST[49] (National Institute of Standards and Technology) with additional support from other US government agencies. Participation in TRECVid has been rising since its early days, and in 2007 54 teams from all over the world took part. Smeaton et al (2006) give an overview of the TREC Video Retrieval Evaluation initiative.

Figure 5.1 shows a typical audiovisual topic of the 2003 TRECVid Interactive Track. Its information need is described as "Find shots from behind the pitcher in a baseball game as he throws a ball that the batter swings at". The images in Figure 5.1 visualise this information need and can be used for a query by example. Other search topics may be exemplified by short video clips or a combination of video clips and images. The 2003 TRECVid test collection repository consists of video shots from mainly US news programmes.

---

[45] http://inex.is.informatik.uni-duisburg.de
[46] http://www.inex.otago.ac.nz
[47] http://trecvid.nist.gov
[48] http://trec.nist.gov
[49] http://www.nist.gov

Figure 5.1: Example pictures supporting TRECVid topic 102: Find shots from behind the pitcher in a baseball game as he throws a ball that the batter swings at

Every year 25 topics are released to all participating groups, who would have pre-processed and indexed the test collection prior to this. The rules for the *interactive task* of the search track allow searchers to spend 15 minutes per topic to find as many relevant shots as possible; they are free to create a search engine query from the given topic in any way they see fit, modify their query, and collect shots that they deem relevant. Each participating group returns the results of their searches to NIST, who are then responsible for assessing the returned shots from all the participating groups. The assessors, often retired intelligence workers, would look at a pool of results for each topic and assess the relevance of each shot in the pool for a topic. In order to be resourceful with the assessors' time, only the union of the top n, say 100, of all the results from different groups for a particular topic is put into this pool. The explicitly assessed shots for each topic form the relevance judgements. Shots that were not assessed during this procedure are those that none of the many participating systems reported in their respective top n results, and the implicit assumption is that these unassessed shots are *not* relevant. The reason for this is the prohibitive cost of assessing all shots against all topics.

This ground truth is then the basis on which participating retrieval systems can be compared. It is possible to use this setting for later evaluation outside the TRECVid programme: the only slight disadvantage is that the assessed algorithm would not have contributed to the pooling process; hence, if the new algorithm uncovered many relevant shots that no other algorithm of the participating groups has reported in their top n results, then these would be treated as irrelevant.

The interactive task is only one task amongst many. There are *manual tasks* where the searchers are allowed to formulate and submit a query *once* for each topics without further modification; there is an *automated task* where the generation of the computer query from a search topic such as in Figure 5.1 is fully automated without any human intervention. These three tasks form the *search track* of the TRECVid evaluation conference, which is one of typically three to five tracks, each year. Over the years other tracks have included:

Shot segmentation, ie, the sectioning of a video into units that result from a single operation of the camera, is a basic but essential task that any video processing unit has to carry out. Hard cuts, where adjacent shots are basically edited by simply concatenating the shots, are relatively easy to detect as the frames of a video change abruptly. Modern editing techniques deploy gradual transmissions, though, eg, fade out/in, which provide continuity between shots and thus are harder to detect. Shot segmentation algorithms vary widely in their efficiency, ie, how much faster (or slower) they are than playing the video. Generally, algorithms that need to decode the video stream into frames tend to be slower than algorithms that operate on the compressed video format.

The *story segmentation* track meant to identify the (news) story boundaries with their time. A news story is defined as a segment of news broadcast with a coherent focus. While a story can be composed of multiple shots (eg, an anchorperson introduces a reporter, who interviews someone in the field and uses archive material to explain background), a single shot can contain story boundaries, e.g. an anchorperson switching to the next news topic. Although this track is non-trivial, it has only been part of TRECVid for a couple of years.

In 2007 TRECVid introduced new video genres taken from a real archive in addition to its previous focus on news: news magazine, science news, news reports, documentaries, educational programming and archival video. The idea was to see how well the video retrieval and processing technologies apply to new sorts of data.

In addition to that, the BBC Archive has provided about 100 hours of unedited material (also known as *rushes*) from five dramatic series to support an exploratory track of *rushes summarisation*: systems should construct a very short video clip that includes the major objects and events of the original video. A dedicated workshop at ACM Multimedia (Over and Smeaton, 2007) presented the results of these efforts.

The *Surveillance event detection* track is a more recent addition to TRECVid that operates on around 150 hours of UK Home Office surveillance data at London Gatwick International Airport.

The *Content-based copy detection* track tries to identify modified segments of a video under a variety of transformations such as a change of aspect ratio, colour, contrast, encoding, bit rate, addition of material, deletion of material, picture in picture in the video part or bandwidth limitation and variate mixing with other audio content in the audio part. Real world applications would be copyright control, de-duplication in large data repositories, grouping of video results in large video repositories or advertisement tracking.

Feature extraction tracks have played an important role throughout the lifetime of TRECVid. Many requests for archival video contain requests for specific features (see above discussion in this section). One of the frequently required aspects is that of a specific camera motion. In the low-level feature extraction version, camera motions such as *pan (left or right)* or *tilt (up or down)* had to be detected. Generally, owing to the semantic gap, high level feature extraction tasks are more difficult. They concern semantic concepts such as *indoor, outdoor, people, face, text overlay, speech* etc. These concepts can be very useful additional search criteria to home in on many real-world requests. Smeaton et al (2009b) have summarised the work done on the TRECVid high-level feature task and show the progress made across the spectrum of various approaches.

5.4.5   IMAGECLEF

ImageCLEF[50] is an evaluation workshop, which is part of the Cross-Language Evaluation Forum (CLEF, pronounce *cle* after the French word for key). The main objective of ImageCLEF is to

---

[50]http://ir.shef.ac.uk/imageclef

advance the field of image retrieval through a sound, metric-based independent evaluation for image information retrieval tasks. The evaluation procedure is modelled after NIST's TREC, possibly owing to the fact that CLEF itself originated from the cross-lingual track of the TREC in 1999.

ImageCLEF started as a new track for the CLEF 2003 edition led by University of Sheffield. Its original task was a pure cross-language retrieval task based on image captions: "given a user need expressed in a language other than English, find as many relevant images as possible". The ImageCLEF tasks changed over the years. In 2004, a medical retrieval task started, in which an example image was used to perform a search against a medical image database consisting of images such as scans and X-rays. The first automatic image annotation task was carried out on medical images, and in 2006 the annotation task was extended to include a photographic collection. The ImageCLEF photo track is also of interest to Geographic Retrieval (see Subsection 5.4.6 below). Since 2006 it has used the IAPR-TC12 corpus[51] containing 20,000 colour photos with associated metadata supplied by Viventura, a holiday company. As the images are all travel photos, the locations that the pictures were taken in is integral to these multimedia documents. There are 60 queries with relevance judgements including 24 queries with geographic constraints.

In 2009 retrieval and annotation tasks over photographic and medical image collections were carried out as well as an image retrieval task over wikipedia images. One new robotic image visual task was introduced, in which participants should determine the location of a robot based on images acquired with a perspective camera mounted on it. Another novelty of the 2009 edition of Image-CLEF was the use of a hierarchical vocabulary, a so-called *ontology*, together with a new hierarchical evaluation metric for the automatic image annotation task.

5.4.6   GEOCLEF

The GeoCLEF[52] track was introduced to the CLEF workshop in 2005 as an ad-hoc TREC style evaluation for geographic Information Retrieval systems; this provided a uniform evaluation for the growing GIR community and is becoming the de facto standard for evaluating GIR systems. GeoCLEF has moved its home to the University of Hildesheim[53].

The GeoCLEF 2005-08 English corpus consists of approximately 135,000 news articles, taken from the 1995 Glasgow Herald and the 1994 Los Angeles Times; the overall corpus also includes German, Spanish and Portuguese documents. There are 100 GeoCLEF queries from 2005–08 (25 from each year). These topics are generated by hand by the four organising groups. Each query is provided with a title, description and narrative. The title and description contain brief details of the query, while the narrative contains a more detailed description including relevance criteria. The 2005 queries have additional fields for concept, spatial relation and location. However, these fields were discarded in later years as unrealistic. Typical topics of GeoCLEF include *Shark Attacks off Australia and California* (Topic 001) or the rather more difficult *Wine regions around rivers in Europe* (Topic 026). Mandl et al (2008) present an overview of GeoCLEF 2007.

---

[51]http://www.imageclef.org/photodata
[52]http://ir.shef.ac.uk/geoclef
[53]http://www.uni-hildesheim.de/geoclef

5.4.7   MIREX

The MIREX[54] (Music Information Retrieval Evaluation eXchange) is a TREC-style evaluation effort organised by the International Music Information Retrieval Systems Evaluation Laboratory (IMIRSEL[55]) at the Graduate School of Library and Information Science, of the University of Illinois at Urbana-Champaign. It is a community-based evaluation conference for Music Information Retrieval systems and algorithms. Downie (2008) looks at the background, structure, challenges, and contributions of MIREX and provides some insights into the state-of-the-art in Music Information Retrieval research as a whole.

5.5   MULTIMEDIA SEARCH AND MINING SYSTEMS

The state-of-the-art in multimedia indexing is still very much a text-based business, for example, piggy-back search of text that is associated with multimedia: all the modern available tools for building platforms for indexing are centred around text: the C++ library Lemur[56] for language modelling and text search, the open-source JAVA Lucene[57] text search engine are two examples.

Yet, specifically for content-based multimedia search (exemplified by the search by example paradigm) the uptake in industry has been very low. A notable exception is Virage[58], a project suite owned by Autonomy. Virage brings together complementary technologies from multimedia, security and infrastructure specialists. Virage make the claim to offer a product set capable of television, video, audio and CCTV challenges of any kind, ie, from making television content fully searchable and accessible via IPTV to supplying and managing complex security systems.

In an attempt to overcome boundaries to market for multimedia analysis (as opposed to text analysis), the Commission of the European Communities invited consortia at the end of 2005 to bid for joint projects specifically in the area of audio-visual search engines. This section presents PHAROS (5.5.1), VITALAS (5.5.2) and TRIPOD (5.5.3), all projects that started early 2007.

5.5.1   PHAROS

PHAROS[59] (Platform for searching of audiovisual resources across online spaces) is an EU-funded integrated project (2007–2009), coordinated by Engineering Ingegneria Informatica SpA of Italy. The PHAROS project builds a next generation audiovisual search platform, to be designed, developed and applied jointly by a consortium of 13 academic and industrial players, including 3 small and medium enterprises.

The PHAROS mission (Debald et al, 2006; Bozzon et al, 2009) is to move business scenarios in the audiovisual domain from a point-solution search engine paradigm to an integral search platform paradigm taking future user and search requirements as key design principles. The platform

---

[54]http://www.music-ir.org/mirex
[55]http://music-ir.org/evaluation
[56]http://www.lemurproject.org
[57]http://lucene.apache.org
[58]http://www.virage.com
[59]http://www.pharos-audiovisual-search.eu

allows modular application development, enables knowledge sharing and technology integration, code and skill reuse. PHAROS has advanced the state of the art in the audiovisual domain, including novel content-publishing mechanisms, automated semantic annotation, advanced query brokering integrating schema-agnostic and content-based search, context-awareness and personalization, innovative user interfaces, content protection and spam detection.

5.5.2   VITALAS

VITALAS[60] (Video and image Indexing and Retrieval in the Large Scale) is an EU-funded integrated project (2007–2009), led by GEIE ERCIM, France. VITALAS is an innovative project designed to provide advanced solutions for indexing, searching and accessing large scale digital audiovisual content. The focus of this initiative is the application of advanced technology to real use-cases that reflect the expectations and concerns of major European multimedia archives. VITALAS addresses three main challenges: cross-media indexing (automated annotation) and retrieval; large scale search techniques; and visualisation and context adaptation (personalized services considering both online and offline).

5.5.3   TRIPOD

TRIPOD[61] (TRI-Partite multimedia Object Description) is an EU-funded integrated project, coordinated by the University of Sheffield (2007–2009). TRIPOD aims to develop a series of techniques, which significantly and rapidly advance both the quality and breadth of search results returned from image collections. The project assumes that location plays a key role in image retrieval. Another key aspect is the creation of a large and diverse collection of geo-referenced photographs, which are used for testing. TRIPOD automatically builds rich multi-faceted text and semantic descriptions of the landscape and permanent man-made features pictured in a photograph, builds captions in a range of different languages and automatically updates captions when new information about a location becomes available.

5.6   BROWSING AND PRESENTATION

Even when a world of information has been reduced to a subset that is appropriate to a particular need or query, there still remains the problem of presenting the data to a user in a meaningful and useful way. A number of active projects are looking at new ways to organise and present data with the aim of helping the user to quickly digest the relevant information, and to combine it with additional sources where appropriate.

---

[60]http://vitalas.ercim.org
[61]http://tripod.shef.ac.uk

5.6.1   ÜBASE

The aim of üBase[62] (Heesch et al, 2004) is to create a web-based image and video browser for content-based retrieval that integrates the current research into browsing and searching into a unified interface. The resulting browser provides the user with the power to browse a large image collection quickly and accurately.

The project's main focus was on the important issues of integrating the searching and browsing mechanisms, thereby improving the user experience. The browser seamlessly integrates the following main features: search with relevance feedback, browsing results by rank; hierarchical browsing; lateral browsing using NN^k networks; temporal browsing; historical browsing and image/video viewer.

5.6.2   SPIRIT

SPIRIT[63] (Spatially-Aware Information Retrieval on the Internet) (Jones et al, 2002) was a research project funded by the EU for the period of 2002–2005. It was a collaborative effort with six European partners, coordinated by Cardiff University, UK. The project has been engaged in the design and implementation of a search engine to find documents and datasets on the web relating to places or regions referred to in a query. The project has created software tools and techniques that can be used to produce search engines and websites that display intelligence in the recognition of geographical terminology. In order to demonstrate and evaluate the project outcomes, a spatially-aware prototype search engine has been built and is serving as the platform for testing and evaluation of new techniques in geographical information retrieval.

5.6.3   MSPACE

The mSpace[64] project at the University of Southampton. mSpace is an interaction model and software framework to help people access and explore information (schraefel et al, 2006) thereby helping to build knowledge from exploring those relationships. mSpace does this by offering several powerful tools for organizing an information space to suit a person's interest: slicing, sorting, swapping, infoViews and preview cues. mSpace presents several associated categories from an information space, and then lets users manipulate how many of these categories are presented and how they are arranged. In this way, people can organize the information to suit their interests, while concurrently having available to them multiple other complementary paths through that information.

5.7   IMAGINATION IS THE ONLY LIMIT

The project discussed above are not in any way fully representative of all the research and development that goes on in multimedia information retrieval. New and noteworthy ideas and applications come up all the time.

---

[62] http://ubase.open.ac.uk
[63] http://www.geo-spirit.org
[64] http://mspace.fm

For example, Kitamura et al (2008) analyse food images with a view to estimate and log the balance of food in the photo in terms of grains, vegetables, mean & beans, fruit and milk. The same research team was amongst one of the first who took an interest in life-long recording of one's life. Aizawa et al (2001) experimented with video cameras attached to the clothes that record all the time. One of the big research questions here is how to summarise 80 years of video, as it is impossible to watch it all. Puangpakisiri et al (2008) experimented with wearing and logging two devices: a SensCam, which frequently takes pictures (some 1000 per day), and a WiFi positioning device, eg, through a mobile phone. They were able to classify many activities, such as walking, shopping, travelling, eating with a high precision.

There are interesting ideas using multimedia to connect children with cultural heritage, requiring a browsing and access system without using keywords: Yamada et al (2006) developed such a system which they named CEAX[65] (across cultures, educational scenes and digital archives).

Music information retrieval has its own set of fascinating work from drum pattern retrieval through voice percussion (Nakano et al, 2004) to thumbnailing music with colour pattern according to acoustic features (Yoshii and Goto, 2008) or building active-listening interfaces that allow you to display virtual dancers that are synchronised with the music; to change the timbre of instrument sounds on CD recordings; to browse large music collections; to change drum sound and patterns during music playback and more (Goto, 2007).

These few examples demonstrate that imagination is the only limit of research in multimedia information retrieval.

5.8   EXERCISES

5.8.1   SEARCH TYPES CONTINUED

Coming back to Exercises 1.6.5 and 2.6.1, pick a few research projects in this chapter that interest you most and determine which search modes of Figure 1.6 on page 6 have been deployed there.

5.8.2   OVERVIEW DIAGRAM OF PROJECTS

In this chapter, I have categorised and discussed interesting multimedia information retrieval projects along the dimensions *multimedia representation and management*; *digital libraries*; *metadata and automated annotation*; *user needs and evaluation*; *multimedia search and mining systems*; and *browsing and presentation of multimedia data*. Some projects show aspects of more than component, though.

Look through the projects and determine whether or not they have an important aspect in (m) multimedia-specific search and representation, (d) digital libraries and metadata or (u) user-centric approaches (eg, through browsing or recognition of workflow needs). Each project can cover one to three aspects. Draw an intersecting Venn diagram of the three overlapping project sets (m), (d) and (u). Which areas are over-represented, which ones under-represented?

---

[65]http://ceax.nii.ac.jp

CHAPTER 6

Summary

This book has introduced basic concepts of multimedia information retrieval technologies for a number of different query and document types; these were the piggy-back text search, automated annotation, content-based retrieval and fingerprinting. The discussed paradigms include summarising complex multimedia objects such as TV news, information visualisation techniques for document clusters, visual search by example, relevance feedback and methods to create browsable structures within the collection. These exploration modes share three common features: they are automatically generated, depend on visual senses and interact with the user of the multimedia collections.

Multimedia information retrieval has its very own challenges mainly in the semantic gap and in the polysemy that is inherently present in under-specified query-by-example scenarios. I have given some examples of user-centred methods that support information retrieval in multimedia digital libraries. Each of these methods can be seen as an alternative mode to the traditional digital library management tools of metadata and classification. The new visual modes aim at generating a multi-faceted approach to present digital content: *video summaries* as succinct versions of media that otherwise would require a high bandwidth to display and considerable time by the user to assess; *information visualisation* techniques help the user to understand a large set of documents that match a query; *visual search* and *relevance feedback* afford the user novel ways to express their information need without recourse to verbal descriptions that are bound to be language-specific; alternative retrieval modes such as *lateral browsing* and *geo-temporal browsing* will allow users to explore collections using lateral associations and geographic or temporal filters rather than following strict classification schemes that seem more suitable for trained librarians than the occasional user of multimedia collections. The cost for these novel approaches will be low, as they are automated rather than human-generated.

Multimedia information retrieval is by far not a closed area as is demonstrated by the selection of recent research projects in Chapter 5. I envisage that the constant progress of research in this area will make accessible digital multimedia resources with less metadata and at lower cost. I predict that multimedia information retrieval will bring about a much closer interlinked digital and physical world, for example, through applications that use images or recordings from the real world to link to digital resources: a snippet of a song will be a viable way to the opening times of movies that feature the song; a picture of leaves will be an easy path to information about the corresponding plant from a database; a snapshot of a building as query on a camera mobile phone will result in tourist information about its significance.

Acknowledgements. The paradigms outlined in this book and their implementations would not have been possible without the ingenuity, imagination and hard work of all the people I am fortunate to work with or to have worked with: Paul Browne, Matthew Carey, Abdigani Diriye, Shyamala Doraisamy, Eric Fernandez, Daniel Heesch, Peter Howarth, Rui Hu, Qiang Huang, Zi Huang, Partha Lal, Suzanne Little, Hai-Ming Liu, Ainhoa Llorente, João Magalhães, Alexander May, Simon Overell, Marcus Pickering, Adam Rae, Edward Schofield, Shalini Sewraz, Dawei Song, Lawrence Wong, Alexei Yavlinsky, Srdan Zagorac and Jianhan Zhu.

I am grateful for the UK's Engineering and Physical Sciences Research Council (EPSRC) support, who have partially sponsored writing this book through their grant *Video Digital Libraries* (EP/G036187/1) while collaborating with David Bainbridge at the University of Waikato from Nov 2008 to Apr 2009. Some of the work reported here was funded in part by EU's Sixth Framework Programme through the integrated project PHAROS (IST-2006-045035). Another EPSRC grant, Multimedia Knowledge Management Network[1] (GR/T02690/01, 2004–2008), has enabled me to interact with colleagues and learn about their respective fields and perspectives. In particular, I am grateful for discussions with Kiyoharu Aizawa, University of Tokyo; David Bainbridge, Waikato University; Peter Bruza, Queensland University of Technology; Greg Crane, Tufts University; Hamish Cunningham, University of Sheffield; David Dawson, Museums, Libraries and Archives Council; John Eakins, Northumbria University; Peter Enser, University of Brighton; Frederic Fol Leymarie, Goldsmiths, University of London; David Forsyth, University of California at Berkeley; Mickaël Gardoni, Université du Québec; Masataka Goto, AIST, Japan; Cathal Gurrin, Dublin City University; Alex Hauptmann, Carnegie Mellon University; Ian Horrocks, Oxford University; Ebroul Izquierdo, Queen Mary, University of London; Joemon Jose, Glasgow University; Steve Jupe, BBC Archives; Noriko Kando, National Institute of Informatics, Japan; Mounia Lalmas, Glasgow University; Hyowon Lee, Dublin City University; Paul Lewis, University of Southampton; George Mallen, Systems Simulations Ltd; R Manmatha, University of Massachusetts at Amherst; Wolfgang Nejdl, University of Hanover; Maja Pantic, Imperial College London; Alan Payne, Kodak Research Cambridge; Mark Plumbley, Queen Mary, University of London; Stefan Poslad, Queen Mary, University of London; Keith van Rijsbergen, Glasgow University; Shin'ichi Satoh, National Institute of Informatics, Japan; Thomas Seidl, RWTH Aachen; Mark Sanderson, University of Sheffield; Mark Sandler, Queen Mary, University of London; Alan Smeaton, Dublin City University; Steffen Staab, University of Koblenz-Landau; Jonathan Teh, Motorola Labs; Chris Wilkie, BBC Archives; Ian Witten, Waikato University; Ken Wood, Microsoft Research Cambridge; Li-Qun Xu, BT Group; Roelof van Zwol, Yahoo Research Europe; and countless others. All credit goes to these, while I take all blame for misrepresentations and errors.

Stefan Rüger

---

[1] http://www.mmkm.org

Credits

Fig 1.1: *Cuneiform script tablet*, the Kirkor Minassian collection in the Library of Congress, ca 24th century BCE

Fig 1.2: *Text index*, DK Eyewitness Travel Guides, New Zealand, Dorling Kindersley, 2001 — reprinted 2002

Fig 1.3: *Peace Pagoda*, Milton Keynes, Stefan Rüger, July 2007

Fig 1.4: *Snap.Send.Get*^{TM}, with kind permission from Snaptell Inc

Fig 1.5: *Medical-image retrieval (mock-up)* based on existing üBase search engine, see Fig 4.8, with modifications by Peter Devine

Fig 1.6: *New search engine types* graphic design by Peter Devine

Fig 1.7: *Queen and Booby Moore*, © Associated Press/Empics, used with permission

Fig 1.8: *Woman and columns*, Århus Art Museum, Stefan Rüger, May 1996

Fig 1.9: *Memex design*, redrawn by Jon Linney based on `http://www.kerryr.net/pioneers` (2 June 2008) from a drawing originally found in Life Magazine, November 19, 1945, p 123

Fig 2.1: Spoof library card created by Harriett Cornish, Nov 2009

Fig 2.5: *Music retrieval video*, Music Retrieval System Interface and Video Production, Shyamala Doraisamy and Kok Huai Meian, University Putra Malaysia; MIDI files from `http://www.classicalarchives.com`; Bach's Fugue No.1 in C major BWV 846; voice: Kok Huai Meian; humming: Shyamala Doraisamy; used with permission

Figs 2.7, 2.9 and 2.10: Royalty-free images from Corel Gallery 380,000, © Corel Corporation, all rights reserved

Fig 2.11: *Behold*, by Alexei Yavlinsky, screenshots from `http://photo.beholdsearch.com`, 19 July 2007, now `http://www.behold.cc` with thumbnails of creative-commons Flickr images

Fig 2.12: Screenshot of audacity programme `http://audacity.sourceforge.net`

Fig 3.3: *3d colour histogram visualisation* by Anuj Kumar, May 2008

Fig 3.4: *Textures*, Stefan Rüger, June 2008

Fig 3.5: *Texture computation programme* by Peter Howarth, 2004

Fig 4.1: Screenshot of *ANSES*, originally written by Marcus Pickering, 2000, modified by Lawrence Wong, 2004; the images and part of the text displayed were recorded from British Broadcasting Corporation, `http://www.bbc.co.uk`

Fig 4.2: *Anticipation*, a film by Vlad Tanasescu with Claudio Baldassarre, Silvia Cassese, Sohan Jheeta and the voice of Samuel Spycher; lights and production by Chris Valentine; music: Johannes Brahms, Op.45 Ein deutsches Requiem "Denn alles Fleisch, es ist wie Gras", the Holden Consort Orchestra and Choir; media: Statue of Liberty and World Trade Centre picture 1 from National Park Service at `http://www.nps.gov`, Statue of Liberty and World Trade Centre picture 2 from Marvin at `http://www.flickr.com`; objects by Ernest von Rosen at `http://www.amgmedia.com`

Fig 4.3: *Visualisation of shot boundary detection* by Marcus Pickering, May 2008

Fig 4.4: *Keyframe computation with hive2*, a shot boundary detection programme by Marcus Pickering, 2000, modified by Eric Fernandez, 2007

Fig 4.5: *Sammon map* interface designed and written by Matthew Carey

Fig 4.6: *Dendro map* interface designed and written by Daniel Heesch

Fig 4.7: *Radial visualisation* interface designed and written by Matthew Carey

Fig 4.8: *üBase* written 2004 by Alexander May with back-end components by Daniel Heesch, Peter Howarth, Marcus Pickering and Alexei Yavlinsky; later modified by Paul Browne

Figs 4.8 and 4.9: Thumbnails from royalty-free images from Corel Gallery 380,000, © Corel Corporation, all rights reserved

Fig 4.10: *uInteract* interface by Haiming Liu and Srdan Zagorac; images from ImageCLEF 2007 competition `http://www.clef-campaign.org` (Grubinger et al, 2006)

Figs 4.11 and 4.12: *üBase* see Fig 4.8; thumbnails and full frame in the (partial) screenshots from videos of the TREC Video Retrieval Evaluation 2003 dataset, `http://trecvid.nist.gov`

Fig 4.13: *View of the world from 9th Avenue*, drawing by Saul Steinberg, *The New Yorker 29* March 1976, © 2010 The Saul Steinberg Foundation/Artists Rights Society (ARS), New York, and © Condé Nast Publications

Figs 4.14 and 4.15: *Heat world map video and images*, Simon Overell using wikipedia and NASA maps from Blue Marble: Next Generation, NASA's Earth Observatory

Fig 4.16: *Cartograms*, Simon Overell using the application MAPresso from `http://www.mapresso.com`

Fig 4.17: *Geotemporal browsing* screenshot by Simon Overell

Fig 4.18: *NewsRoom* interface by Abdigani Diriye, 2009, based on a back-end by Eric Fernandez, 2006

Fig 4.20: *View of the world from Piccadilly Circus* with kind permission from Jon Linney, May 2008, free after Saul Steinberg's *New Yorker* cover of 29 March 1976

Fig 5.1: images reproduced from TREC Video Retrieval Evaluation 2003, `http://trecvid.nist.gov`

Page 157: Photograph by Chris Valentine, processed by Harriett Cornish

Bibliography

M Addis, M Boniface, S Goodall, P Grimwood, S Kim, P Lewis, K Martinez and A Stevenson (2003). SCULPTEUR: towards a new paradigm for multimedia museum information handling. In *International Semantic Web Conference*, pp 582–596. Springer LNCS 2870. DOI: 10.1007/b14287. 5.2.3

M Addis, K Martinez, P Lewis, J Stevenson and F Giorgini (2005). New ways to search, navigate and use multimedia museum collections over the web. In *Museums and the Web 2005: Archives and Museum Informatics*. 5.2.3

C Aggarwal, A Hinneburg and D Keim (2001). On the surprising behavior of distance metrics in high dimensional space. In *International Conference on Database Theory*, pp 420–434. Springer LNCS 1973. DOI: 10.1007/3-540-44503-X_27. 3.3.1

C Aggarwal and P Yu (2000). The IGrid index: reversing the dimensionality curse for similarity indexing in high dimensional space. In *ACM International Conference on Knowledge Discovery and Data Mining*, pp 119–129. DOI: 10.1145/347090.347116. 3.5

L von Ahn and L Dabbish (2004). Labeling images with a computer game. In *ACM International Conference on Human Factors in Computing Systems*, pp 319–326. DOI: 10.1145/985692.985733. 2.4, 5.3

K Aizawa, K Ishijima and M Shiina (2001). Summarizing wearable video. In *International Conference on Image Processing*, pp 398–401. DOI: 10.1109/ICIP.2001.958135. 5.7

M Ankerst, D Keim and H Kriegel (1996). Circle segments: a technique for visually exploring large multidimensional data sets. In *IEEE Visualization*. 4.2

L Armitage and P Enser (1997). Analysis of user need in image archives. *Journal of Information Science 23*(4), 287–299. DOI: 10.1177/016555159702300403. 5.4

P Au, M Carey, S Sewraz, Y Guo and S Rüger (2000). New paradigms in information visualisation. In *ACM International Conference on Research and Development in Information Retrieval*, pp 307–309. DOI: 10.1145/345508.345610. 4.2

M Baillie and J Jose (2004). An audio-based sports video segmentation and event detection algorithm. In *IEEE International Conference on Computer Vision and Pattern Recognition*, pp 110. DOI: 10.1109/CVPR.2004.298. 2.4

B Bartell, G Cottrell and R Belew (1994). Automatic combination of multiple ranked retrieval systems. In *ACM International Conference on Research and Development in Information Retrieval*, pp 173–181. 3.6.1

J Beis and D Lowe (1997). Shape indexing using approximate nearest-neighbour search in high-dimensional spaces. In *IEEE International Conference on Computer Vision and Pattern Recognition*, pp 1000–1006. DOI: 10.1109/CVPR.1997.609451. 3.5

R Bellman (1961). *Adaptive control processes: a guided tour*. Princeton University Press. 3.5

K Beyer, J Goldstein, R Ramakrishnan and U Shaft (1999). When is "nearest neighbor" meaningful? In *International Conference on Database Theory*, pp 217–235. Springer LNCS 1540. DOI: 10.1007/3-540-49257-7_15. 3.5

W Birmingham, R Dannenberg and B Pardo (2006). Query by humming with the VocalSearch system. *Communications of the ACM 49*(8), 49–52. DOI: 10.1145/1145287.1145313. 2.2

A Blandford, A Adams, S Attfield, G Buchanan, J Gow, S Makri, J Rimmer and C Warwick (2008). The PRET A Rapporter framework: evaluating digital libraries from the perspective of information work. *Information Processing & Management 44*(1), 4–21. DOI: 10.1016/j.ipm.2007.01.021. 5.2

A Blandford, S Keith, I Connell and H Edwards (2004). Analytical usability evaluation for digital libraries: a case study. In *ACM/IEEE Joint Conference on Digital Libraries*, pp 27–36. DOI: 10.1145/996350.996360. 5.2

A Blandford and H Stelmaszewska (2002). Usability of musical digital libraries: a multimodal analysis. In *International Symposium on Music Information Retrieval*, pp 231–237. 5.2

D Blei and M Jordan (2003). Modeling annotated data. In *ACM International Conference on Research and Development in Information Retrieval*, pp 127–134. DOI: 10.1145/860435.860460. 2.4

K Börner (2000). Visible threads: a smart VR interface to digital libraries. In *International Symposium on Electronic Imaging 2000: Visual Data Exploration and Analysis*, pp 228–237. DOI: 10.1117/12.378899. 4.2

A Bozzon, M Brambilla, P Fraternali, F Nucci, S Debald, E Moore, W Neidl, M Plu, P Aichroth, O Pihlajamaa, C Laurier, S Zagorac, G Backfried, D Weinland and V Croce (2009). PHAROS: an audiovisual search platform. In *ACM International Conference on Research and Development in Information Retrieval*, pp 841. DOI: 10.1145/1571941.1572161. 5.5.1

A Bradley and F Stentiford (2003). Visual attention for region of interest coding in JPEG2000. *Journal of Visual Communication and Image Representation 14*, 232–250. DOI: 10.1016/S1047-3203(03)00037-3. 5.1

A Broder (1997). On the resemblance and containment of documents. In *Compression and Complexity of Sequences*, pp 21–29. DOI: 10.1109/SEQUEN.1997.666900. 2.5.2, 2.5.2

V Bush (1945). As we may think. *The Atlantic Monthly 176*(1), 101–108. Reprinted in http://dx.doi.org/10.1145/227181.227186.

D Cai and C van Rijsbergen (2005). Semantic relations and information discovery. In D Ruan, G Chen, E Kerre and G Wets (Eds), *Intelligent data mining: techniques and applications*, pp 79–102. Springer. DOI: 10.1007/11004011_4. 5.1

J Calic, N Campbell, S Dasiopoulou and Y Kompatsiaris (2005). An overview of multimodal video representation for semantic analysis. In *European Workshop on the Integration of Knowledge, Semantics and Digital Media Technology*, pp 39–45. 5.1

I Campbell (2000). Interactive evaluation of the ostensive model using a new test collection of images with multiple relevance assessments. *Journal of Information Retrieval 2*(1), 89–114. DOI: 10.1023/A:1009902203782. 4.4

P Cano, E Batlle, T Kalker and J Haitsma (2005). A review of audio fingerprinting. *41*(3), 271–284. DOI: 10.1007/s11265-005-4151-3. 2.5.1

S Card (1996). Visualizing retrieved information: a survey. *IEEE Computer Graphics and Applications 16*(2), 63–67. DOI: 10.1109/38.486683. 4.2

M Carey, D Heesch and S Rüger (2003). Info navigator: a visualization interface for document searching and browsing. In *International Conference on Distributed Multimedia Systems*, pp 23–28. 4.2, 5.2.4

A Cavallaro (2004). Adding privacy constraints to video-based applications. In *European Workshop on the Integration of Knowledge, Semantics and Digital Media Technology*. 5.1

A Cavallaro and T Ebrahimi (2004). Interaction between high-level and low-level image analysis for semantic video object extraction. *Journal on Applied Signal Processing 2004*(6), 786–797. DOI: 10.1155/S1110865704402157. 2.4

A Chakravarthy, F Ciravegna and V Lanfranchi (2006). AKTiveMedia: cross-media document annotation and enrichment. In *International Semantic Web Conference*. 5.1

B Chawda, B Craft, P Cairns, S Rüger and D Heesch (2005). Do "attractive things work better"? An exploration of search tool visualisations. In *BCS Human-Computer Interaction Conference*, Volume 2, pp 46–51. 4.2

H-L Chen (2001). An analysis of image queries in the field of art history. *Journal of the American Society for Information Science and Technology 52*(3), 260–273. DOI: 10.1002/1532-2890(2000)9999:9999<::AID-ASI1606>3.3.CO;2-D. 5.4

Y Choi and E Rasmussen (2002). Users' relevance criteria in image retrieval in American history. *Information Processing & Management 38*(5), 695–726. DOI: 10.1016/S0306-4573(01)00059-0. 5.4

M Christel, A Hauptmann, A Warmack and S Crosby (1999). Adjustable filmstrips and skims as abstractions for a digital video library. In *IEEE Forum on Research and Technology Advances in Digital Libraries*, pp 98–104. DOI: 10.1109/ADL.1999.777702. 4.1

M Christel, J Richardson and H Wactlar (2006). Facilitating access to large digital oral history archives through informedia technologies. In *ACM/IEEE Joint Conference on Digital libraries*, pp 194–195. DOI: 10.1145/1141753.1141795. 5.2.2

M Christel and A Warmack (2001). The effect of text in storyboards for video navigation. In *IEEE International Conference on Acoustics, Speech, and Signal Processing*, pp 1409–1412. DOI: 10.1109/ICASSP.2001.941193. 4.1

R Cilibrasi and P Vitányi (2007). The Google similarity distance. *IEEE Transactions on Knowledge and Data Engineering 19*(3), 370–383. DOI: 10.1109/TKDE.2007.48. 3.3.6

P Clough and M Sanderson (2004). Relevance feedback in cross language image retrieval. In *European Conference on Information Retrieval*, pp 238–252. Springer LNCS 2997. DOI: 10.1007/b96895. 4.3

A Cockburn and J Savage (2003). Comparing speed-dependent automatic zooming with traditional scroll, pan and zoom methods. In *BCS Human-Computer Interaction Conference*, pp 87–102. 4.5.2

L Cooniss, A Ashford and M Graham (2000). Information seeking behaviour in image retrieval. VISOR 1 final report. Technical report, Library and Information Commission Research Report, British Library. 5.4

L Cooniss, J Davis and M Graham (2003). A user-oriented evaluation framework for the development of electronic image retrieval systems in the workplace: VISOR 2 final report. Technical report, Library and Information Commission Research Report, British Library. 5.4

K Cox (1992). Information retrieval by browsing. In *International Conference on New Information Technology*, pp 69–80. 4.4

K Cox (1995). *Searching through browsing*. PhD thesis, University of Canberra. 4.4

N Cristianini and J Shawe-Taylor (2000). *An introduction to support vector machines*. Cambridge University Press. 5.3

N Cristianini, J Shawe-Taylor and H Lodhi (2002). Latent semantic kernels. *Journal of Intelligent Information Systems 18*(2), 127–152. DOI: 10.1023/A:1013625426931. 5.3.2

B Croft and T Parenty (1985). A comparison of a network structure and a database system used for document retrieval. *Information Systems 10*, 377–390. DOI: 10.1016/0306-4379(85)90042-0. 4.4

H Cunningham (2002). GATE, a general architecture for text engineering. *Computers and the Humanities 36*, 223–254. DOI: 10.1023/A:1014348124664. 4.1

H Cunningham, D Maynard, K Bontcheva and V Tablan (2002). GATE: a framework and graphical development environment for robust nlp tools and applications. In *Association for Computational Linguistics*. 5.1.1

A Dalby (1986). The Sumerian catalogs. *Journal of Library History 21*(3), 475–487. 1.1

M Datar, N Immorlica, P Indyk and V Mirrokni (2004). Locality-sensitive hashing scheme based on *p*-stable distributions. In *ACM Annual Symposium on Computational Geometry*, pp 253–262. DOI: 10.1145/997817.997857. 2.5.2

R Datta, D Joshi, J Li and J Wang (2008). Image retrieval: ideas, influences, and trends of the new age. *ACM Computing Surveys 40*(2), 1–60. DOI: 10.1145/1348246.1348248. 2.3

D Dearholt and R Schvaneveldt (1990). Properties of Pathfinder networks. In R Schvaneveldt (Ed), *Pathfinder associative networks: studies in knowledge organization*, pp 1–30. Norwood. 4.4

S Debald, W Nejdl, F Nucci, R Paiu and M Plu (2006). PHAROS — platform for search of audiovisual resources across online spaces. In *International Conference on Semantics and Digital Media Technology*. 5.5.1

A del Bimbo and P Pala (1997). Visual image retrieval by elastic matching of user sketches. *IEEE Transactions on Pattern Analysis and Machine Intelligence 19*(2), 121–132. DOI: 10.1109/34.574790. 3.2.4

T Deselaers, D Keysers and H Ney (2008). Features for image retrieval: an experimental comparison. *Information Retrieval 11*(2), 77–107. DOI: 10.1007/s10791-007-9039-3. 3.2

S Dietze, A Gugliotta and J Domingue (2007). Towards adaptive e-learning applications based on semantic web services. In *TENCompetence Open Workshop on Service Oriented Approaches and Lifelong Competence Development Infrastructures*. 5.1.9

S Dietze, A Gugliotta and J Domingue (2009). Supporting interoperability and context-awareness in e-learning through situation-driven learning processes. *International Journal of Distance Education Technologies 7*(2), 20–43. 5.1.9

S van Dongen (2000). A cluster algorithm for graphs. Technical Report INS-R0010, National Research Institute for Mathematics and Computer Science in the Netherlands. 4.4

S Doraisamy (2005). *Polyphonic music retrieval: the n-gram approach*. PhD thesis, Imperial College London. 2.2

M Dowman, V Tablan, H Cunningham and B Popov (2005). Web-assisted annotation, semantic indexing and search of television and radio news. In *International World Wide Web Conference*, pp 225–234. DOI: 10.1145/1060745.1060781. 4.1

S Downie (2008). The music information retrieval evaluation exchange (2005-2007): a window into music information retrieval research. *Acoustical Science and Technology 29*(4), 247–255. DOI: 10.1250/ast.29.247. 5.4.7

S Downie and M Nelson (2000). Evaluation of a simple and effective music information retrieval method. In *ACM International Conference on Research and Development in Information Retrieval*, pp 73–80. DOI: 10.1145/345508.345551. 2.2

P Duygulu, K Barnard, N de Freitas and D Forsyth (2002). Object recognition as machine translation: learning a lexicon for a fixed image vocabulary. In *European Conference on Computer Vision*, pp 349–354. Springer LNCS 2353. DOI: 10.1007/3-540-47979-1_7. 2.4

P Enser (1993). Query analysis in a visual information retrieval context. *Journal of Document and Text Management 1*(1), 25–52. 5.4

P Enser and C McGregor (1992). Analysis of visual information retrieval queries. Technical report, British Library Research and development Report 6104. 5.4

P Enser and C Sandom (2002). Retrieval of archival moving imagery — CBIR outside the frame? In *International Conference on Image and Video Retrieval*, pp 85–106. Springer LNCS 2383. DOI: 10.1007/3-540-45479-9_22. 2.4, 5.4.2

P Enser and C Sandom (2003). Towards a comprehensive survey of the semantic gap in visual image retrieval. In *International Conference on Image and Video Retrieval*, pp 163–168. Springer LNCS 2728. DOI: 10.1007/3-540-45113-7_29. 2.4

J Farquhar, D Hardoon, H Meng, J Shawe-Taylor and S Szedmak (2005). Two view learning: SVM-2K, theory and practice. In *Neural Information Processing Systems*. 5.3.3

S Feng, R Manmatha and V Lavrenko (2004). Multiple Bernoulli relevance models for image and video annotation. In *IEEE International Conference on Computer Vision and Pattern Recognition*, pp 1002–1009. DOI: 10.1109/CVPR.2004.1315274. 2.4

R Fowler, B Wilson and W Fowler (1992). Information navigator: an information system using associative networks for display and retrieval. Technical Report NAG9-551, 92-1, Department of Computer Science, University of Texas. 4.4

H Freeman (1961). On the encoding of arbitrary geometric configurations. *IEEE Transactions on Electronic Computers 10*(2), 260–268. DOI: 10.1109/TEC.1961.5219197. 3.2.4

C Frost and A Noakes (1998). Browsing images using broad classification categories. In *American Society for Information Science SIGCR Classification Research Workshop*, pp 71–79. 5.4

M Gardoni, E Blanco and S Rüger (2005). MICA-Graph: a tool for managing text and sketches during design processes. *Journal of Intelligent Manufacturing 16*, 397–407. DOI: 10.1007/s10845-005-1653-6. 5.1

A Gilliland-Swetland (1998). Defining metadata. In M Baca (Ed), *Introduction to Metadata: Pathways to Digital Information*. Getty Information Institute. 2.1

A Goodrum and A Spink (2001). Image searching on the Excite web search engine. *Information Processing & Management 37*(2), 295–311. DOI: 10.1016/S0306-4573(00)00033-9. 5.4

M Goto (2007). Active music listening interfaces based on signal processing. In *IEEE International Conference on Acoustics, Speech, and Signal Processing*, Volume 4, pp 1441–1444. DOI: 10.1109/ICASSP.2007.367351. 5.7

J Gracia and E Mena (2008). Web-based measure of semantic relatedness. In *International Conference on Web Information Systems Engineering*, pp 136–150. Springer LNCS 5175. DOI: 10.1007/978-3-540-85481-4_12. 3.3.6

M Grubinger, P Clough, H Müller and T Deselaers (2006). The IAPR TC-12 benchmark: a new evaluation resource for visual information systems. In *International Workshop OntoImage 2006 Language Resources for Content-based Image Retrieval*, pp 13–23. 6

A Guttman (1984). R-trees: a dynamic index structure for spatial searching. In *ACM International Conference on Management of Data*, pp 47–57. DOI: 10.1145/971697.602266. 3.5

J Haitsma and T Kalker (2003). A highly robust audio fingerprinting system with an efficient search strategy. *Journal of New Music Research 32*(2), 211–221. DOI: 10.1076/jnmr.32.2.211.16746. 2.5.1, 2.5.1, 2.5.1

D Hardoon, C Saunders, S Szedmak and J Shawe-Taylor (2006). A correlation approach for automatic image annotation. In *International Conference on Advanced Data Mining and Applications*, pp 681–692. Springer LNCS 4093. DOI: 10.1007/11811305_75. 5.3.3

D Hardoon, S Szedmak and J Shawe-Taylor (2004). Canonical correlation analysis: an overview with application to learning methods. *Neural Computation 16*, 2639–2664. DOI: 10.1162/0899766042321814. 5.3.3

J Hare and P Lewis (2004). Salient regions for query by image content. In *International Conference on Image and Video Retrieval*, pp 264–268. Springer LNCS 3115. DOI: 10.1007/b98923. 2.4

J Hare and P Lewis (2005). Saliency-based models of image content and their application to auto-annotation by semantic propagation. In *Multimedia and the Semantic Web Workshop at the European Semantic Web Conference*. 2.4

J Hare, P Lewis, P Enser and C Sandom (2006). Mind the gap: another look at the problem of the semantic gap in image retrieval. In *Multimedia Content Analysis, Management and Retrieval, SPIE Vol 6073*, pp 1–12. DOI: 10.1117/12.647755. 2.4

S Hastings (1995). Query categories in a study of intellectual access to digitized art images. In *American Society for Information Science*. 5.4

A Hauptmann (2005). Lessons for the future from a decade of Informedia video analysis research. In *International Conference on Image and Video Retrieval*, pp 1–10. Springer LNCS 3568. 5.2.2

A Hauptmann, J Gao, R Yan, Y Qi, J Yang and H Wactlar (2004). Automated analysis of nursing home observations. *Pervasive Computing 3*(2), 15–21. DOI: 10.1109/MPRV.2004.1316813. 5.2.2

A Hauptmann, W-H Lin, R Yan, J Yang and M-Y Chen (2006). Extreme video retrieval: joint maximization of human and computer performance. In *ACM Conference on Multimedia*, pp 385–394. DOI: 10.1145/1180639.1180721. 5.2.2

A Hauptmann, R Yan, W-H Lin, M Christel and H Wactlar (2007). Can high-level concepts fill the semantic gap in video retrieval? A case study with broadcast news. *IEEE Transactions on Multimedia 9*(5), 958–966. DOI: 10.1109/TMM.2007.900150. 5.2.2

D Heesch (2005). *The NN^k technique for image searching and browsing*. PhD thesis, Imperial College London. 4.4

D Heesch, P Howarth, J Magalhães, A May, M Pickering, A Yavlinsky and S Rüger (2004). Video retrieval using search and browsing. In *TREC Video Retrieval Evaluation*. 5.6.1

D Heesch, M Pickering, S Rüger and A Yavlinsky (2003). Video retrieval using search and browsing with key frames. In *TREC Video Retrieval Evaluation*. 4.4

D Heesch and S Rüger (2003). Relevance feedback for content-based image retrieval: what can three mouse clicks achieve? In *European Conference on Information Retrieval*, pp 363–376. Springer LNCS 2633. DOI: 10.1007/3-540-36618-0_26. 4.3, 4.3

D Heesch and S Rüger (2004). NN^k networks for content based image retrieval. In *European Conference on Information Retrieval*, pp 253–266. Springer LNCS 2997. DOI: 10.1007/b96895. 4.4

D Heesch and S Rüger (2005). Image browsing: semantic analysis of NN^k networks. In *International Conference on Image and Video Retrieval*, pp 609–618. Springer LNCS 3568. DOI: 10.1007/11526346_64. 5.1

M Hemmje, C Kunkel and A Willet (1994). LyberWorld — a visualization user interface supporting fulltext retrieval. In *ACM International Conference on Research and Development in Information Retrieval*, pp 249–259. 4.2, 4.2

X Hilaire and J Jose (2007). Enhancing CBIR through feature optimization, combination and selection. In *International Workshop on Content-based Multimedia Indexing*, pp 267–274. DOI: 10.1109/CBMI.2007.385421. 5.1

F Hillier and G Lieberman (1990). *Introduction to mathematical programming*. McGraw-Hill. 3.3.4

D Hillmann and E Westbrooks (Eds) (2004). *Metadata in practice*. American Library Association. 2.1

P Hoffman, G Grinstein and D Pinkney (1999). Dimensional anchors: a graphic primitive for multidimensional multivariate information visualizations. In *New Paradigms in Information Visualisation and Manipulation in conjunction with ACM CIKM*, pp 9–16. DOI: 10.1145/331770.331775. 4.2

L Hollink, A Schreiber, B Wielinga and M Worring (2004). Classification of user image descriptions. *International Journal of Human Computer Studies 61*(5), 601–626. DOI: 10.1016/j.ijhcs.2004.03.002. 5.4

F Hopfgartner, J Urban, R Villa and J Jose (2007). Simulated testing of an adaptive multimedia information retrieval system. In *International Workshop on Content-based Multimedia Indexing*, pp 328–335. DOI: 10.1109/CBMI.2007.385430. 4.3

P Howarth and S Rüger (2005a). Fractional distance measures for content-based image retrieval. In *European Conference on Information Retrieval*, pp 447–456. Springer LNCS 3408. DOI: 10.1007/b107096. 2.5.2, 3.3.1

P Howarth and S Rüger (2005b). Robust texture features for still-image retrieval. *IEE Proceedings on Vision, Image and Signal Processing 152*(6), 868–874. DOI: 10.1049/ip-vis:20045185. 3.2.3, 5.1

P Howarth and S Rüger (2005c). Trading precision for speed: localised similarity functions. In *International Conference on Image and Video Retrieval*, pp 415–424. Springer LNCS 3568. DOI: 10.1007/11526346_45. 3.5

R Hu, S Rüger, D Song, H-M Liu and Z Huang (2008). Dissimilarity measures for content-based image retrieval. In *IEEE International Conference on Multimedia and Expo*, pp 1365–1368. DOI: 10.1109/ICME.2008.4607697. 3.3.1

M Huebscher and J McCann (2008). A survey of Autonomic Computing — degrees, models, and applications. *ACM Computing Surveys 40*(3), 1–28. DOI: 10.1145/1380584.1380585. 5.1

International Commission on Illumination (1986). CIE colorimetry. 3.7.3

S Intner, S Lazinger and J Weihs (2006). *Metadata and its impact on libraries.* Westport, CT: Libraries Unlimited. DOI: 10.1336/1591581451. 2.1

J Jeon, V Lavrenko and R Manmatha (2003). Automatic image annotation and retrieval using cross-media relevance models. In *ACM International Conference on Research and Development in Information Retrieval*, pp 119–126. DOI: 10.1145/860435.860459. 2.4

H Joho and J Jose (2008). Effectiveness of additional representations for the search result presentation on the web. *Information Processing & Management 44*(1), 226–241. DOI: 10.1016/j.ipm.2007.02.004. 5.4.1

C Jones, R Purves, A Ruas, M Sanderson, M Sester, M van Kreveld and R Weibel (2002). Spatial information retrieval and geographical ontologies: an overview of the SPIRIT project. In *ACM International Conference on Research and Development in Information Retrieval*, pp 387–388. DOI: 10.1145/564376.564457. 5.6.2

M Jones, W Harwood, D Bainbridge, G Buchanan, D Frohlich, D Rachovides, M Frank and M Lalmas (2008). "Narrowcast yourself": designing for community storytelling in a rural Indian context. In *ACM Conference on Designing Interactive Systems*, pp 369–378. DOI: 10.1145/1394445.1394485. 5.2.7

C Jörgensen and P Jörgensen (2005). Image querying by image professionals: research articles. *Journal of the American Society for Information Science and Technology 56*(12), 1346–1359. DOI: 10.1002/asi.v56:12. 5.4

D Keim, J Schneidewind and M Sips (2004). CircleView: a new approach for visualizing time-related multidimensional data sets. In *Conference on Advanced Visual Interfaces*, pp 179–182. ACM. DOI: 10.1145/989863.989891. 4.2

L Keister (1994). User types and queries: impact on image access systems. In R Fidel, T Hahn, E Rasmussen and P Smith (Eds), *Challenges in Indexing Electronic Text and Images*. Learned Information, Inc. 5.4

Y Kim and S Ross (2007). Searching for ground truth: a stepping stone in automated genre classification. In *DELOS Conference on Digital Libraries: Research and Development*, pp 248–261. Springer LNCS 4877. DOI: 10.1007/978-3-540-77088-6_24. 5.3

Y Kim and S Ross (2008). Examining variations of prominent features in genre classification. In *Hawaiian Conference on System Sciences*. IEEE. DOI: 10.1109/HICSS.2008.157. 5.3

K Kitamura, T Yamasaki and K Aizawa (2008). Food log by analyzing food images. In *ACM Conference on Multimedia*, pp 999–1000. DOI: 10.1145/1459359.1459548. 5.7

Z Kong and M Lalmas (2007). Using XML logical structure to retrieve (multimedia) objects. In *European Conference on Digital Libraries*, pp 100–111. Springer LNCS 4675. DOI: 10.1007/978-3-540-74851-9_9. 5.1

R Korfhage (1991). To see or not to see — is that the query? In *ACM International Conference on Research and Development in Information Retrieval*, pp 134–141. DOI: 10.1145/122860.122873. 4.2

C Lagoze and S Payette (2000). Metadata: principles, practices and challenges. In A Kenney and O Rieger (Eds), *Moving Theory into Practice: Digital Imaging for Libraries and Archives*, Mountain View, CA. Research Libraries Group. 2.1

C Lagoze and H Van de Sompel (2003). The making of the open archives initiative protocol for metadata harvesting. *Library Hi Tech 21*(2), 118–128. DOI: 10.1108/07378830310479776. 5.2

M Lalmas (2009). *XML retrieval.* Synthesis Lectures on Information Concepts, Retrieval, and Services. Morgan & Claypool Publishers. DOI: 10.2200/S00203ED1V01Y200907ICR007. 2.1

V Lavrenko, R Manmatha and J Jeon (2003). A model for learning the semantics of pictures. In *Neural Information Processing Systems*, pp 553–560. 2.4

F Lerner (2001). *The story of libraries: from the invention of writing to the computer age.* Continuum International Publishing Group. 1.1

V Levenshtein (1966). Binary codes capable of correcting deletions, insertions and reversals. *Soviet Physics — Doklady 10*(8), 707–710. Translated from *Doklady Akademii Nauk SSSR, 163(4),* pp 845–848, 1965. 3.3.6

M Lew, N Sebe, C Djeraba and R Jain (2006). Content-based multimedia information retrieval: state of the art and challenges. *ACM Transactions on Multimedia Computing, Communications, and Applications 2*(1), 1–19. DOI: 10.1145/1126004.1126005. 2.3

W-H Lin and A Hauptmann (2008). Identifying news broadcasters' ideological perspectives using a large-scale video ontology. In *International Language Resources for Content-based Image Retrieval Workshop.* 5.2.2

S Little and S Rüger (2009). Conservation of effort in feature selection for image annotation. In *IEEE Workshop on Multimedia Signals Processing.* 3.2

C Liu, J Yuen and A Torralba (2009a). Nonparametric scene parsing: label transfer via dense scene alignment. In *IEEE International Conference on Computer Vision and Pattern Recognition*, pp 1972–1979. DOI: 10.1109/CVPRW.2009.5206536. 2.4

H-M Liu, V Uren, D Song and S Rüger (2009b). A four-factor user interaction model for content-based image retrieval. In *International Conference on the Theory of Information Retrieval*, pp 297–304. Springer LNCS 5766. DOI: 10.1007/978-3-642-04417-5_29. 4.3

H-M Liu, S Zagorac, V Uren, D Song and S Rüger (2009c). Enabling effective user interactions in content-based image retrieval. In *Asia Information Retrieval Symposium*. 4.3

Y Liu, J Yang and A Hauptmann (2007). Undirected graphical models for video analysis and classification. In *IEEE International Conference on Multimedia and Expo*, pp 1495–1498. DOI: 10.1109/ICME.2007.4284945. 5.1

Z Liu, Y Wang and T Chen (1998). Audio feature extraction and analysis for scene segmentation and classification. *VLSI Signal Processing 20*(1–2), 61–79. DOI: 10.1023/A:1008066223044. 3.2.6

H Lodhi, G Karakoulas and J Shawe-Taylor (2002a). Boosting strategy for classification. *Journal of Intelligent Data Analysis 6*(2), 149–174. 5.3

H Lodhi, C Saunders, J Shawe-Taylor, N Cristianini and C Watkins (2002b). Text classification using string kernels. *Journal of Machine Learning Research 2*, 419–444. 5.3.2

D Lowe (1999). Object recognition from local scale-invariant features. In *IEEE International Conference on Computer Vision*, Volume 2, pp 1150–1157. DOI: 10.1109/ICCV.1999.790410. 3.2.5

D Lowe (2004). Distinctive image features from scale-invariant keypoints. *International Journal of Computer Vision 60*(2), 91–110. DOI: 10.1023/B:VISI.0000029664.99615.94. 3.2.5

J Magalhães and S Rüger (2006). Logistic regression of semantic codebooks for semantic image retrieval. In *International Conference on Image and Video Retrieval*, pp 41–50. Springer LNCS 4071. DOI: 10.1007/11788034_5. 2.4

J Magalhães and S Rüger (2007). Information-theoretic semantic multimedia indexing. In *International Conference on Image and Video Retrieval*, pp 619–626. DOI: 10.1145/1282280.1282368. 2.4, 5.1

A Makadia, V Pavlovic and S Kumar (2008). A new baseline for image annotation. In *European Conference on Computer Vision*, pp 316–329. Springer LNCS 5304. DOI: 10.1007/978-3-540-88690-7_24. 2.4

T Mandl, F Gey, G Di Nunzio, N Ferro, R Larson, M Sanderson, D Santos, C Womser-Hacker and X Xie (2008). GeoCLEF 2007: the CLEF 2007 cross-language geographic information retrieval track overview. In *Advances in Multilingual and Multimodal Information Retrieval*, pp 745–772. Springer LNCS 5152. DOI: 10.1007/978-3-540-85760-0_96. 5.4.6

M Markkula and E Sormunen (2000). End-user searching challenges indexing practices in the digital newspaper photo archive. *Information Retrieval 1*(4), 259–285. DOI: 10.1023/A:1009995816485. 5.4

J Martinet, Y Chiaramella, P Mulhem and I Ounis (2003). Photograph indexing and retrieval using star-graphs. In *Content Based Multimedia Indexing Conference*. 5.1

K Mc Donald and A Smeaton (2005). A comparison of score, rank and probability-based fusion methods for video shot retrieval. In *International Conference on Image and Video Retrieval*, pp 61–70. Springer LNCS 3568. DOI: 10.1007/11526346_10. 3.6.1

D Messing, P van Beek and J Errico (2001). The MPEG-7 colour structure descriptor: image description using colour and local spatial information. In *International Conference on Image Processing*, Volume 1, pp 670–673. DOI: 10.1109/ICIP.2001.959134. 2.1, 3.2.5

D Metzler and R Manmatha (2004). An inference network approach to image retrieval. In *International Conference on Image and Video Retrieval*, pp 42–50. Springer LNCS 3115. DOI: 10.1007/b98923. 2.4

T Mitchell (1997). *Machine learning*. McGraw Hill. 3.6.2

M Mrak, N Sprljan, G Abhayaratne and E Izquierdo (2004). Scalable generation and coding of motion vectors for highly scalable video coding. In *Picture Coding Symposium*. 5.1

M Muja and D Lowe (2009). Fast approximate nearest neighbors with automatic algorithm configuration. In *International Conference on Computer Vision Theory and Applications*, Volume 1, pp 331–340. 3.5

W Müller and A Henrich (2004). Faster exact histogram intersection on large data collections using inverted VA-files. In *International Conference on Image and Video Retrieval*, pp 455–463. Springer LNCS 3115. DOI: 10.1007/b98923. 3.5

T Nakano, J Ogata, M Goto and Y Hiraga (2004). A drum pattern retrieval method by voice percussion. In *International Conference on Music Information Retrieval*. 5.7

S Nene and S Nayar (1997). A simple algorithm for nearest neighbor search in high dimensions. *IEEE Transactions on Pattern Analysis and Machine Intelligence* 19(9), 989–1003. DOI: 10.1109/34.615448. 3.5

L Onural, T Sikora, J Ostermann, A Smolic, M R Civanlar and J Watson (2006). An assessment of 3DTV technologies. In *NAB Broadcast Engineering Conference*, pp 456–467. 5.1.4

S Ornager (1995). The newspaper image database: empirical supported analysis of users' typology and word association clusters. In *ACM International Conference on Research and Development in Information Retrieval*, pp 212–218. DOI: 10.1145/215206.215362. 5.4

P Over and A Smeaton (Eds) (2007). *TVS 2007: proceedings of the international workshop on TRECVid video summarization*. DOI: 10.1145/1290031. ACM, ISBN 978-1-59593-780-3. 5.4.4

S Overell (2009). *Geographic information retrieval: classification, disambiguation and modelling*. PhD thesis, Imperial College London. 4.5.1

S Overell and S Rüger (2008). Using co-occurrence models for placename disambiguation. *International Journal of Geographical Information Science* 22(3), 265–287. DOI: 10.1080/13658810701626236. 4.5.1

O Oyekoya and F Stentiford (2004). Eye tracking as a new interface for image retrieval. *BT Technology Journal* 22(3), 161–169. DOI: 10.1023/B:BTTJ.0000047130.98920.2b. 4.3

E Persoon and K-S Fu (1977). Shape discrimination using Fourier descriptor. *IEEE Transactions on Systems, Man and Cybernetics* 7(3), 170–179. DOI: 10.1109/TSMC.1977.4309681. 3.2.4

D Petrelli, S Mazumdar, A-S Dadzie and F Ciravegna (2009). Multi visualization and dynamic query for effective exploration of semantic data. In *International Semantic Web Conference*. 5.1.6

M Pickering and S Rüger (2003). Evaluation of key-frame based retrieval techniques for video. *Computer Vision and Image Understanding* 92(2), 217–235. DOI: 10.1016/j.cviu.2003.06.002. 3.6.2

M Pickering, L Wong and S Rüger (2003). ANSES: summarisation of news video. In *International Conference on Image and Video Retrieval*, pp 481–486. Springer LNCS 2728. DOI: 10.1007/3-540-45113-7_42. 4.1

S Potter, Y Kalfoglou, H Alani, M Bachler, S Buckingham Shum, R Carvalho, A Chakravarthy, S Chalmers, S Chapman, B Hu, A Preece, N Shadbolt, A Tate and M Tuffield (2007). The application of advanced knowledge technologies for emergency response. In *International Information Systems for Crisis Response and Management*. 5.1

W Puangpakisiri, T Yamasaki and K Aizawa (2008). High level activity annotation of daily experiences by a combination of a wearable device and wi-fi based positioning system. In *IEEE International Conference on Multimedia and Expo*, pp 1421–1424. DOI: 10.1109/ICME.2008.4607711. 5.7

J Puzicha, T Hofmann and J Buhmann (1997). Non-parametric similarity measures for unsupervised texture segmentation and image retrieval. In *IEEE International Conference on Computer Vision and Pattern Recognition*, pp 267–272. DOI: 10.1109/CVPR.1997.609331. 3.3.3

I Reid and A Zisserman (1996). Goal-directed video metrology. In *European Conference on Computer Vision*, Volume II, London, UK, pp 647–658. Springer LNCS 1065. DOI: 10.1007/3-540-61123-1_178. 3

J Rimmer, C Warwick, A Blandford, J Gow and G Buchanan (2008). An examination of the physical and the digital qualities of humanities research. *Information Processing & Management 44*(3), 1374–1392. DOI: 10.1016/j.ipm.2007.09.001. Corrected proof available online 22 October 2007. 5.2

J Rousu, C Saunders, S Szedmak and J Shawe-Taylor (2006). Kernel-based learning of hierarchical multilabel classification models. *Journal of Machine Learning Research 7*, 1601–1626. 5.3

Y Rubner, C Tomasi and L Guibas (2000). The earth mover's distance as a metric for image retrieval. *International Journal of Computer Vision 40*(2), 99–121. DOI: 10.1023/A:1026543900054. 3.3.4

I Ruthven, M Lalmas and C van Rijsbergen (2003). Incorporating user search behavior into relevance feedback. *Journal of the American Society for Information Science and Technology 54*(6), 529–549. DOI: 10.1002/asi.10240. 4.3

J Rydberg-Cox (2005). The cultural heritage language technologies consortium. *D-Lib Magazine 11*(5). DOI: 10.1045/may2005-rydberg-cox. 5.2.4

J Rydberg-Cox, L Vetter, S Rüger and D Heesch (2004). Approaching the problem of multi-lingual information retrieval and visualization in Greek and Latin and Old Norse texts. In *European Conference on Digital Libraries*, pp 168–178. Springer LNCS 3232. DOI: 10.1007/b100389. 4.2, 5.2.4

A Salway and M Graham (2003). Extracting information about emotions in films. In *ACM Conference on Multimedia*, pp 299–302. DOI: 10.1145/957013.957076. 2.4

A Salway, A Vassiliou and K Ahmad (2005). What happens in films? In *IEEE International Conference on Multimedia and Expo*, pp 4. DOI: 10.1109/ICME.2005.1521357. 2.4

J Sammon (1969). A nonlinear mapping for data structure analysis. *IEEE Transactions on Computers 18*(5), 401–409. DOI: 10.1109/T-C.1969.222678. 4.2

M Sanderson and J Kohler (2004). Analyzing geographic queries. In *Workshop on Geographic Information Retrieval at SIGIR*. 4.5.1

S Santini and R Jain (2000). Integrated browsing and querying for image databases. *IEEE Multimedia 7*(3), 26–39. DOI: 10.1109/93.879766. 4.4

m schraefel, M Wilson, A Russell and D Smith (2006). mSpace: improving information access to multimedia domains with multimodal exploratory search. *Communications of the ACM 49*(4), 47–49. DOI: 10.1145/1121949.1121980. 5.6.3

J Shawe-Taylor and N Cristianini (2002). On the generalisation of soft margin algorithms. *IEEE Transactions on Information Theory 48*(10), 2721–2735. DOI: 10.1109/TIT.2002.802647. 5.3

J Shawe-Taylor and N Cristianini (2004). *Kernel methods for pattern analysis*. Cambridge University Press. 5.3

B Shneiderman, D Feldman, A Rose and X Ferré Grau (2000). Visualizing digital library search results with categorical and hierarchical axes. In *ACM Conference on Digital Libraries*, pp 57–66. DOI: 10.1145/336597.336637. 4.2

B Sigurbjörnsson and R van Zwol (2008). Flickr tag recommendation based on collective knowledge. In *International World Wide Web Conference*, pp 327–336. DOI: 10.1145/1367497.1367542. 5.1.10

P Sinclair, P Lewis, K Martinez, M Addis, D Prideaux, D Fina and G Da Bormida (2005). eCHASE: sustainable exploitation of electronic cultural heritage. In *European Workshop on the Integration of Knowledge, Semantics and Digital Media Technology*. 5.2

R Sinha and M Winslett (2007). Multi-resolution bitmap indexes for scientific data. *ACM Transactions on Database Systems 32*(3), *Article 16*, 1–39. DOI: 10.1145/1272743.1272746. 3.5

A Sinitsyn (2006).   Duplicate song detection using audio fingerprinting for consumer electronics devices.   In *IEEE International Symposium on Consumer Electronics*, pp 1–6. DOI: 10.1109/ISCE.2006.1689403. 2.5

A Smeaton, C Gurrin, H Lee, K Mc Donald, N Murphy, N O'Connor, D O'Sullivan, B Smyth and D Wilson (2004). The Físchlár-news-stories system: personalised access to an archive of TV news. In *RIAO Conference on Coupling Approaches, Coupling Media and Coupling Languages for Information Retrieval*, pp 3–17. 4.1

A Smeaton, P Over and A Doherty (2009a).   Video shot boundary detection: seven years of TRECVid activity.   *Computer Vision and Image Understanding in press*. DOI: 10.1016/j.cviu.2009.03.011. 4.1

A Smeaton, P Over and W Kraaij (2006).   Evaluation campaigns and TRECVid. In *ACM International Workshop on Multimedia Information Retrieval*, pp 321–330. DOI: 10.1145/1178677.1178722. 5.4.4

A Smeaton, P Over and W Kraaij (2009b). High-level feature detection from video in TRECVid: a 5-year retrospective of achievements. In A Divakaran (Ed), *Multimedia Content Analysis: Theory and Applications*, pp 151–174. Springer. DOI: 10.1007/978-0-387-76569-3_6. 5.4.4

A Smeulders, M Worring, S Santini, A Gupta and R Jain (2000). Content-based image retrieval at the end of the early years. *IEEE Transactions on Pattern Analysis and Machine Intelligence 22*(12), 1349–1380. DOI: 10.1109/34.895972. 5.4

J Sussner, L Lohse, M Thomas, G García, I Alonso and A Muñoz (2006).   3d navigable interface for interactive movie Gormenghast Explore.   In *IEEE International Conference on Automated Production of Cross Media Content for Multi-Channel Distribution*, Volume 0, pp 242–250. DOI: 10.1109/AXMEDIS.2006.2. 5.1.3

S Sweeney and F Crestani (2004). Supporting searching on small screen devices using summarisation. In *Mobile and Ubiquitous Information Access*. 5.1

H Tamura, S Mori and T Yamawaki (1978). Textural features corresponding to visual perception. *IEEE Transactions on Systems, Man and Cybernetics 8*(6), 460–472. DOI: 10.1109/TSMC.1978.4309999. 3.2.3, 3.2.3

G Thallinger, G Kienast, O Mayor, C Cullen, R Hackett and J Jose (2009). SALERO: semantic audiovisual entertainment reusable objects. In *International Broadcasting Conference*. 5.1.8

T Tolonen and M Karjalainen (2000). A computationally efficient multi-pitch analysis model. *IEEE Transactions on Speech and Audio Processing 8*(6), 708–716. DOI: 10.1109/89.876309. 2.4

A Tombros, I Ruthven and J Jose (2005). How users assess web pages for information seeking. *Journal of the American Society for Information Science and Technology 56*(4), 327–344. DOI: 10.1002/asi.20106. 5.4

A Torralba and A Oliva (2003). Statistics of natural image categories. *Network: Computation in Neural Systems 14*, 391–412. DOI: 10.1088/0954-898X/14/3/302. 2.4

G Tzanetakis and P Cook (2002). Musical genre classification of audio signals. *IEEE Transactions on Speech and Audio Processing 10*(5), 293–302. DOI: 10.1109/TSA.2002.800560. 2.4

J Urban, J Jose and C van Rijsbergen (2006). An adaptive technique for content-based image retrieval. *Multimedia Tools and Applications 31*(1), 1–28. DOI: 10.1007/s11042-006-0035-1. 4.4

A Vinokourov, J Shawe-Taylor and N Cristianini (2002). Inferring a semantic representation of text via cross-language correlation analysis. In *Neural Information Processing Systems*, pp 1473–1480. 5.3.2

J Voss (2007). Tagging, folksonomy & Co — renaissance of manual indexing? *Computing Research Repository abs/cs/0701072*, 1–12. 4.3

A de Vries, N Mamoulis, N Nes and M Kersten (2002). Efficient k-nn search on vertically decomposed data. In *ACM International Conference on Management of Data*, pp 322–333. DOI: 10.1145/564691.564729. 3.5

T Wallace and P Wintz (1980). An efficient three dimensional aircraft recognition algorithm using normalized Fourier descriptors. *Computer Graphics and Image Processing 13*(2), 99–126. DOI: 10.1016/S0146-664X(80)80035-9. 3.2.4

A Wang (2003). An industrial-strength audio search algorithm. In *International Conference on Music Information Retrieval*, pp 7–13. 2.5.1, 2.5.1

D Watts and S Strogatz (1998). Collective dynamics of 'small-world' networks. *Nature 393*, 440–442. DOI: 10.1038/30918. 4.4

R Weber, H-J Stock and S Blott (1998). A quantitative analysis and performance study for similarity search methods in high-dimensional space. In *International Conference on Very Large Databases*, pp 194–205. 3.5

T Westerveld and R van Zwol (2006). The INEX 2006 multimedia track. In *Comparative Evaluation of XML Information Retrieval Systems, International Workshop of the Initiative for the Evaluation of XML Retrieval*, pp 331–344. Springer LNCS 4518. DOI: 10.1007/978-3-540-73888-6_33. 5.4.3

R White, J Jose, C van Rijsbergen and I Ruthven (2004). A simulated study of implicit feedback models. In *European Conference on Information Retrieval*, pp 311–326. Springer LNCS 2997. DOI: 10.1007/b96895. 4.3

R White, J Jose and I Ruthven (2006). An implicit feedback approach for interactive information retrieval. *Information Processing & Management 42*(1), 166–190. DOI: 10.1016/j.ipm.2004.08.010. 4.3

I Witten and D Bainbridge (2002). *How to build a digital library*. Elsevier Science Inc. 5.2.1

I Witten, D Bainbridge and D Nichols (2010). *How to build a digital library* (2nd ed). Morgan Kaufmann. 2.1, 5.2.1

K Wu, E Otoo and A Shoshani (2004a). On the performance of bitmap indices for high cardinality attributes. In *International Conference on Very Large Databases*, pp 24–35. 3.5

S Wu, F Crestani and F Gibb (2004b). New methods of results merging for distributed information retrieval. In *Recent Research in Multimedia Distributed Information Retrieval*, pp 84–100. 5.1

T Yamada, K Aihara, N Kando, S Fujisawa, Y Uehara, T Baba, S Nagata, T Tojo, Y Hiroshima and J Adachi (2006). CEAX's learning support system to explore cultural heritage objects without keyword search. In *Current Developments in Technology-Assisted Education*, Volume I, Badajoz, Spain, pp 318–. Formatex. 5.7

G-Z Yang, L Dempere-Marco, X Hu and A Rowe (2002). Visual search: psychophysical models and practical applications. *Image and Vision Computing Journal 20*(4), 291–305. DOI: 10.1016/S0262-8856(02)00022-7. 4.3

A Yavlinsky, E Schofield and S Rüger (2005). Automated image annotation using global features and robust nonparametric density estimation. In *International Conference on Image and Video Retrieval*, pp 507–517. Springer LNCS 3568. DOI: 10.1007/11526346. 2.4

K Yoshii and M Goto (2008). Music thumbnailer: visualizing musical pieces in thumbnail images based on acoustic features. In *International Conference on Music Information Retrieval*. 5.7

C Zahn and R Roskies (1972). Fourier descriptors for plane closed curves. *IEEE Transactions on Computers 21*(3), 269–281. DOI: 10.1109/TC.1972.5008949. 3.2.4

M Zeng and J Qin (2008). *Metadata*. New York: Neal-Schuman. 2.1

R van Zwol, G Kazai and M Lalmas (2005). INEX 2005 multimedia track. In *Advances in XML Information Retrieval and Evaluation, International Workshop of the Initiative for the Evaluation of XML Retrieval*, pp 497–510. Springer LNCS 3977. DOI: 10.1007/11766278. 5.4.3

R van Zwol, V Murdock, L Garcia Pueyo and G Ramirez (2008). Diversifying image search with user generated content. In *ACM International Conference on Multimedia Information Retrieval*, pp 67–74. DOI: 10.1145/1460096.1460109. 5.1.10

Author's Biography

STEFAN RÜGER

I am a Professor of Knowledge Media at the Knowledge Media Institute, The Open University, UK, and an Honorary Professor (2009–2014) at the Department of Computer Science, University of Waikato, New Zealand. I hold a diploma in Theoretical Physics (equivalent to MSc) from Freie Universität Berlin and received my PhD (Dr rer nat) from Technische Universität Berlin's Informatik Department for my work on the theory of artificial neural networks. Between 1999 and 2004 I held an EPSRC Advanced Research Fellowship at the Department of Computing of Imperial College London where I carved out my academic career from PostDoc (1997) to Reader in Multimedia and Information Systems (2005). My research has evolved over the years from theory of artificial neural networks over data mining and knowledge management to applications in multimedia search engines. At the Knowledge Media Institute I direct a small Multimedia and Information Systems team. I am still involved in the Multimedia Knowledge Management research network that I helped set up. Currently, I am Principal Investigator for The Open University in the European funded PHAROS project (2007–2009).
Homepage http://people.kmi.open.ac.uk/stefan